The Biography of the Devil

the one and only version
authorized by himself ...   ;-)

Contact: www.HarryEilenstein.de
Harry.Eilenstein@web.de
Harry Eilenstein at youtube

Production and publishing house: BoD – Books on Demand, Norderstedt

ISBN: 9783756801039

for Axel Büdenbender

Table of Contents

1.   Who or What is the Devil?

First of all, one can find many different opinions on whether the devil exists at all – and basically none of these opinions can really be substantiated. But the word "devil" triggers all kinds of feelings in almost everyone.

The question of who or what the devil is is important, if only because of the emotional connotation of this topic, but also because even today many people believe in the existence of the devil:

> In 1997, about 25% of the people in the USA believed in the devil; in 2009, it was 26%; in 2013, it was even 57% in one survey.

> In 2002, 23% of people in Germany believed in the devil; in 2019, it was 20%, or 25% in another survey; in 2021, it was 20%.

So we can say that about a quarter of people in Western Christian civilization believe in the existence of the devil.

This raises many questions:

> Is he a remnant from the Neolithic worldview?
> Is he simply the Greek god Pan?
> Is he a mythological figure from the monotheistic religions?
> Is he the god of the pagans?
> Is he the Antichrist?
> Is he the archetype of the rebel?
> Is he the seducer of evil deeds?
> Is he a real being?
> Is he the secret ruler of events on earth?
> Why is he nowhere depicted as a woman?

However, since the stories about the devil are, on the one hand, very diverse and, on the other hand, have changed significantly over the millennia, a "history of the devil" can be written – or, to put it more personally, a "biography of the devil".

1st Dream Journey to the Devil

There is also the possibility to make a dream journey to the devil and to see what one experiences. Since on the one hand dream journeys lead into the subconscious and on the other hand telepathy and telekinesis are the "eye" and the "hand" of the subconscious, it could be that one discovers things by such dream journeys, which one would not have found out otherwise.

Of course, one should not simply believe what one experiences on dream journeys as "reality", but check the experienced for its plausibility – but almost every dream journey is worthwhile, since one finds as good as always also something unexpected, which broadens one's own horizon.

One can also argue about whether one actually talks to the devil on such dream journeys or not. However, the answer to this question is actually not of too much importance, because the essential question is whether one receives meaningful information on these dream journeys and whether one can develop and become healed by them.

This effect they have in any case … and if also the devil can help with one's own healing – why not?

Therefore now follows the first "interview" with the devil:

"Hello devil …"
"Hello Harry."
"I would like to write a book about you, so first of all about what I have found out about your history over the decades. I'd like you to have your say, too – especially since I certainly don't know everything about you. What do you think?"
"Let's see …"
"Is there anything you'd like to tell about yourself?"
"Asshole!"
"Um … why?"
"You don't really want to see me! You're secretly afraid of me!"
"Um … is that an allusion to the evocation I made with Axel a good 40 years ago at a nighttime crossroads in the woods?"
"That alone would be enough."
"All right – then I'll tell you this: After I met Axel, he accepted me as a sorcerer's apprentice …"
"Don't be so long-winded – tell the actual thing and that's it!"
"Alright, if you want – this was supposed to be a short version already … So I drew the prescribed circles and symbols on the crossroads with chalk, then took my divining rod (and held it the wrong way around) and then at midnight summoned the

demon Astaroth – one of the devils from hell. At first nothing happened, then red lights floated over the path to the right of us, then a bright blue flash of light crackled in the tree above us on the left, someone invisible kept coughing between Axel and me, and it began to smell of sulfur, and the presence of someone could be clearly felt in front of the circle.

Then it all became too much for me and I said that I wanted to stop. Then I said the spell and we went back through the forest, but the smell of sulfur remained and so did the coughing of the invisible man between Axel and me. Then we cast the spell again, after which the sulfur smell and the coughing stopped.

When Axel and I separated in the city, I hardly knew where to go because of fear. At home I locked my room, left the light on and hid under the covers.

There I realized that either the fear gets me or I get the fear. So I went to the crossroads in the woods every day until I could lie there in the grass, completely relaxed, and think of something completely different."

"Look – there I gave you a gift: you met your fear and you learned to deal with it. If you hadn't learned that back then, your psyche would have been in shambles afterwards."

"A rather scorpionic method ..."

"It worked after all – what more do you want?"

"Much later I found out that the name 'Astaroth' is a derivative of the goddess name 'Astarte'. This name, like the name 'Isis', comes from the Neolithic 'Aset' in Göbekli Tepe, which means 'sitting one'. Aset was the mother goddess of that time, who sat on the panther throne in the early Neolithic temples. That Axel and I just invoked Astaroth was probably no coincidence, since I got my greatest trauma from an experience with my mother."

"I am fear,
 I am panic,
 I am trauma,
 I am madness,
 I am loss of self...
 I am darkness,
 I am that which you fear,
 I am your shadow,
 I am the figure with the billowing black cloak,
 I am the archetype of the Black Riders and the Dementors –
 I am the repressed,
 I am that which comes from beyond,
 I bring death and destruction...
 ... at least that is your image of me ..."

"And that's not quite true?"

"No ... really not ... even though I am quite also what you have made me to be."

"Hm ... do you want to say more about it?"

"Later ..."

"Thank you."

"That's all right ... it's nice for a change to talk to someone who isn't afraid of me ..."

"Ho!"

2. Goat Horns and Horse's Foot

The images of the devil are all pretty similar:

- he is a man,

- he has goat horns,

- he has billy goat legs or a horse's foot,

- sometimes he has shaggy billy goat legs,

- he often has thick eyebrows, a pointed upper lip and prominent facial features, which suggests that he has a Scorpio Ascendant, and

- he spreads sulfur smell, which also suggests a Scorpio Ascendant, since people with Scorpio Ascendant seem to like this smell.

To grasp this animal symbolism, one must go back very far – to at least the late Paleolithic, i.e. the last phase of the Ice Age between 50,000 and 10,000 BC. During this time, Homo sapiens migrated from Africa to Eurasia and met Homo erectus and Neanderthal there – which led to an intercultural exchange that initiated many new developments.

It is possible, however, that the origins of devil symbolism go back much further into the Paleolithic period to possibly a million years ago. The exact age of these roots, however, is not very important for understanding the history of the devil.

The names of animals were probably something like adjectives in the early language of man. For example, a fast, strong and successful hunter was "like a panther", that is, a "panther". This could be represented and at the same time magically strengthened by wearing the hide of a panther. Also the cave paintings from the late Old Stone Age can be "read" in this way.

The most important "adjectives", which can be found in later times with the same meaning in mythology, are listed below. Among them are also some "adjectives" which are not animals:

- <u>mother</u>: protection, security, backing, knowledge, help

- <u>hill</u> (sweat lodge): pregnancy belly (mother)

- <u>mother's milk</u>: food, warmth, survival

- large carnivore (panther, lion, tiger, cougar, leopard, jaguar, bear, orca, etc.): great power, strength, hunting success

- herd animal (mammoths, reindeer, cattle, horses, wild boar, sheep, goats, gazelle, antelope, etc.): procreative power, fertility, children, family, community

- bird: experience of near-death, hovering over one's own body, astral body, soul

- tree trunk: body

- bird pole (pole with bird on top) and totem pole (large bird pole): pole = body; bird = soul → "Every person has a soul."

- water (springs, lakes, swamps, marshes, sea, etc.): the inaccessible place = otherworld, underworld

- water bird (stork, goose, duck, crane, ibis, etc.): soul in water underworld

- red: blood, life, life force (often represented by red ocher, with which one painted oneself and objects)

- red water bird (flamingo): living ancestors in the afterlife

- flocks of birds (ravens, crows, flamingos, geese, ibises, etc.): community of ancestral spirits

- snake: ancestors in the underworld (snakes live on earth and in the earth, i.e. in caves, crevices, etc.), way to the underworld; blessing of the ancestors, which they send up from the underworld = Kundalini

- fox: cunning, otherworld guide

- canids (wolf, jackal, dog etc.): guardian, helper

- fish: beings in the water underworld, ancestors

- otter: beings in the water underworld, ancestors, especially the sun in the water underworld

Obviously, the symbolism of herd animals is important for the story of the devil – after all, he has goat horns and goat legs or a horse's foot.

There has been another simile, that is, another symbolism early on: the arrival of people in this world is a birth, so the arrival of the dead in the afterlife should be a second birth, that is, a rebirth. As is generally known, birth is preceded by procreation and followed by breastfeeding – this was also known by the people in the Paleolithic Age.

So the dead had to procreate himself again in the hereafter. With whom? Obviously with the greatest archetype of the people (and the mammals in general): with the "great mother". She has been, before she becomes the rebirth-mother, the reprocreation-lover of the dead, and after that then his nursling-fostress.

In the course of time, ritual potions have developed from this nursing: the milk of the Egyptian goddess Hathor in the afterlife, the haoma of the Persians, the soma amrita ("immortality potion") of the Indians, the nectar amrita ("immortality honey potion") of the Greeks, the mead of the Germanic and Celtic gods, the balché of the Mayas, the elixir of life of the alchemists in Europe and India, etc.

Because of the symbolism of reprocreation, after a while, of course, the fear arose that one might have potency problems after one's death and then not be able to reprocreate. What to do? Well, the creatures with the greatest procreative power were obviously the herd animals, which always appear in large flocks. So, in order to secure the procreative power of the dead man, a male herd animal was killed and the dead man was wrapped in the hide of this animal when he was buried, in order to transfer its potency to him – a "magic Viagra", so to speak.

This identification led to the idea of animal/human hybrids, i.e. strictly speaking man/animal hybrids. This whole symbolism applies only to men – to the rebirth of women there seems to have been no symbolism.

During the rebirth of the dead the Great Mother, i.e. the goddess of the beyond, had to take the same animal form as the dead, because otherwise a unification would have been difficult. These motives are still found in the mythology of the later time, in which there was already a written tradition.

The following myths are only a very small selection especially from the Indo-Europeans and the peoples in the Mediterranean area – just because the figure of the devil originated in this area.

> mammoth: It is uncertain, but well conceivable that the huts from the Old Stone Age, which were built completely from mammoth skulls, were understood as the belly of the mammoth goddess, as with the sweat lodge, thus as the belly of the Great Mother in the form of a mammoth.

> cow: Already from the Old Stone Age representations of men with bull head and of women, who hold a cow horn in the hand and look on it, as well as many figures, which represent flowing transitions from cow to woman, are known.

> In Sumer, the sky god An in bull form united with the earth goddess Inanna in cow form, whereupon she gave birth to a calf. In Babylon, Inanna was

given the name "Ishtar" – she was also a cow goddess. In neighboring Elam, a woman with a cow's head was worshipped.

In Egypt, the sky goddesses Hathor and Nut often had the shape of a cow – Hathor was also the rebirth goddess. The grain god and rebirth god Osiris took the form of the bull god Apis during his afterlife journey. A dead man who had successfully reincarnated was called "Ka-mut-ef", i.e. "bull of his mother", i.e. "who has united with his mother" (united = procreation; mother = the reborn soul was the son of the goddess, who has been his lover during the procreation).

From Crete the Minotaur is well known: a man with a bull's head.

Among the Hittites in today's central Turkey the sungod in bull form united with the cow-goddess Pinkir and was reborn as a calf. Among the Lydians neighboring them, Artemis was the cow goddess.

Among the Greeks, Zeus is known as a bull and Io as a cow. The motif of the union of the dead with the mother goddess ("with his mother") led them to the Oedipus theme.

The sacred cows from India are known to almost everyone.

Among the Persians, the sun-god Mithras is also the bull-god. The sungod-godfather had with almost all Indo-European peoples at his nocturnal reincarnation, which preceded his rebirth in the morning, the shape of a bull. With the Slavs the bull god was called "Veles".

Among the Balts Mara was the cow goddess and among the Romans Juno. Among the Celts the bull god is called "Tarvus Trigaranus" and the cow goddess "Damona".

With the Teutons he is called "Jörmunrek" and she "Audhumbla".

The cattle symbolism is widespread in the Mediterranean area and in Europe, because in historical times the cattle was the largest herd animal there.

Finally, Pte-san-win, i.e. the "White Buffalo Woman" is the most important goddess of the Dakota Indians.

horse: The horse symbolism has changed a lot among the Indo-Europeans, because the horses played a big role in their warlike everyday life. The Indo-European sungod-godfather Dhyaus takes the form of a stallion when he is reincarnated, and the mother-goddess takes the form of a mare. Their two children appear in most Indo-Europeans as the horse-twins pulling the chariot of their father, i.e. the sungod, across the sky.

The procreation symbolism is clearest in Demeter and Poseidon, who father a winged horse in the form of a mare and a stallion. The winged horse is a combination of horse and soul-bird, that is, the reborn soul. Among the

Greeks, the horse-shaped dead also appear as centaurs, satyrs and silenas, and the mare goddess also as Selene.

Among the Celts, Belenus is the horse-shaped sungod – Rhiannon, Epona, Etain, Boann and Damona are the horse goddesses.

Among the Germanic people the horse goddess is called Sinmara and Huldar and the horse-shaped reborn sungod Sleipnir.

In the old Indian coronation ritual the queen united as a representative of the mother goddess with the stallion sacrificed for the prospective king, while the king symbolically stayed in the hereafter and waited for his rebirth after this ritual-symbolic reincarnation.

donkey: Probably the donkey transformation in the novel "Metamorphoses" of the Greek poet Ovid is not only a humorous variant of the horse and cattle transformation, because the Greek sungod Apollon is known to have donkey's ears sometimes.

stag: From the Old Stone Age a painting of a man with stag antlers is known (Southern France) and from the New Stone Age a stag mask (Rhineland, Germany). These stag masks have been widespread and are also found in, among other places, Butan, in Central America and in North America.

With the Celts the deer god was called Cernunnos – the deer goddess was called Sirona.

Among the Germanic tribes the hind has no name, but she is the nurse of Sigurd (Siegfried), who is the sungod transferred into the saga. From the Teutons is also known the sun-stag and his two stag-sons.

Among the Hittites the motif of the sun god as a stag was very popular.

The stag motif has been preserved especially by the sun-stag of St. Hubert. Here this symbolism has been transferred to Christ: the sungod Tyr of the Germanic tribes has often been equated to Christ as the sun – and Christ has been the rebirth god of the time.

pig: The pig symbolism has also been widespread in connection with the procreation. It shows up most clearly with the Teutons as Freyr and Freya as well as with the Celts as Lugh and Brigid.

sheep: The sheep is probably strongly underrepresented in the myths as a "poor man's sacrificial animal" and will have been much more widespread in the burial rituals than the myths suggest.

Among the Germanic tribes, the former sun god Heimdall and also his antagonist Loki are found in ram form – Loki sometimes wears ram-horns on his head. The sheep goddess was called "Guma".

The "Golden Fleece" of the Greek Saga is a sungod symbol of the Hittites –

the wooly hide of a ram, that is of golden colour, i.e. the colour of the sun.

From the Egyptians the ram god Chnum is well known.

goat: The dead man as a goat is known from Sumer as "Enki", from the Greeks as "Pan", from the Celts as "Bugius", from the Slavs as "Porewit" and from the Romans as "Faunus". The goat goddess is only found among the Germanic tribes as Heidrun and as Freya.

Probably the goat like the sheep as the "poor people's sacrificial animal" is much underrepresented in the myths.

capricorn: In Sumer the god Enki also appears as a Capricorn.

gazelle and antelope: In Egypt the gazelle goddess Anuket and the antelope goddess Satet were worshipped.

astrology: From these herd animal motives the names of the three zodiac signs Aries (ram), Taurus (bull) and Capricorn are derived.

It shows up thus that the origin of the goat horns and the goat legs and/or the horse foot of the devil lie in this procreation symbolism. Strictly speaking, the beginning of the devil-symbolism was thus the potency-failure-anxiety of the men at the reproduction in the hereafter – without successful reproduction no rebirth in the hereafter … the absolute end. So this potency failure fear was at the same time a death fear …

A violent combination – and against this the animal transformation should help. So the devil has originally once been the magical helper against the fear of failure during the reprocreation. Therefore the devil is always male.

2nd Dream Journey to the Devil

"What do you say to what I have written, devil?"
"Do you want to hire me as an editor or reviewer? You can go whistle for that!"
"Is the development I have described correct?"
"Why do you ask? You are already convinced that it is correct."
"Hm, yes, I am ... I've thought and researched a lot about it ... but your own opinion on it would be quite dear to me, because I'm not so presumptuous to think that I already have it all figured out."
"Fuck you!"
"Now is that to be taken as an approval of the reproreation?"
"Bullshit! If you don't have a real request, then stop bothering me!"

"Fine – I want to know if you are the evil one."

"Of course! What else would it be? Evil is always what you don't want, what you fear, what frightens you. Why do you think I am a figure of death and pain and torture? That is what you fear. I am your shadow, I am what you run away from, what you fight against, what you try to avoid, what you banish instead of looking at. Is there a difference between 'evil' and 'fear'? It's the same thing: you fear something and don't want to have it, so you call it evil. What does 'evil' mean? It just means that you don't want it."

"And that changes over time ..."

"For the Indians, the Germanic tribes, and many other peoples organized as tribes, it was a badge of honor if a man killed another man, or better yet many other men, in battle – today murder is the worst act. Slavery used to be normal – today it is outlawed. For some peoples sex with multiple partners is perfectly normal – for others it is punishable by death. What is evil? There is no 'evil' except what you call it, what you make it, what you don't want. Your will is what creates evil – evil is simply what you do not want. I am your anti-will, your anti-desire, your anti-need. Without you, I would not exist."

"Hm ... yes ... that was very clear now ... thank you."

I just hear the devil grumbling to himself ....

It is strange to thank the devil.

"Ho!"

3. Death and Devil

"Death and the devil" are the two dreaded archetypes. They are the two most feared cards in the Tarot as well – possibly along with the "Tower", symbolizing the destruction and collapse that occurs when you have built something based on false assumptions.

Death as a goat-man and generally as a herd-animal-man is created in connection with death – and the devil dwells in the afterlife. So the devil is closely related to death.

Our image of the grim "reaper" for death comes from an ancient parable from the early Neolithic period. After agriculture was developed in northern Mesopotamia about 8500 BC, people began to describe the cultivation of grain with a simile to man:

- sowing   = procreation
- germination = birth
- growing   = life
- harvest   = death
- storage   = hereafter
- sowing   = (re)procreation
- germination = (re)birth
    … … …

By the fact that this simile was represented in a pictorial way, the motive of the ancestor connected with the motive of the grain to the "grain man". He then became the graingod and the god of the dead like e.g. the Egyptian Osiris.

By the annual repetition procreation and birth became a reprocreation and a rebirth. This suggested that people are also reborn – not only in the afterlife as souls, but in this world as physical people. This image for reincarnation, of course, does not show that reincarnation is not true, but only how the image for it came to be.

This simile was still supplemented by the analogy to the course of the sun:

- sowing	= procreation	= spring	= morning	= east
- germination	= birth	= spring	= morning	= east
- growing	= life	= summer	= noon	= south
- harvest	= death	= autumn	= evening	= west
- storage	= beyond	= winter	= night	= north
- sowing	= procreation	= spring	= morning	= east
- germination	= birth	= spring	= morning	= east

This shows, among other things, that the afterlife is assigned to the night – appropriately enough, the devil is usually summoned at midnight.

A closer look at these old ideas about the "life after death" shows that there is a mistake:

The image of rebirth was initially used to describe only the arrival of the soul in the afterlife – as an image, this is fine. But if one concludes from this that this rebirth must be preceded by a reprocreation, this is not a conclusion from a concrete observation, but a conclusion from a picture. Reprocreation is an extension of a pictorial description, which lacks any concrete basis.

A mythe should always be a description of experiences and observations that is as accurate and precise as possible – only then can it be "real" and helpful.

So, at the root of the origin of the devil there is also another error: The herd-animal-man has been created to solve a problem which does not exist in reality at all – there is no reprocreation really …

This has not been the only error in connection with death which appears in the myths.

One wondered where the souls might be after death, since, as a rule, one did not meet them again. Just as the arrival in the afterlife after death was compared to a second birth, that is, to a rebirth, so it was imagined that after death the souls went to a fertile land (Egyptians), to a paradise-garden (Bibel), to a palace under the earth (Sumer), to the happy hunting grounds (Indians), to a kind of second world (Celts), to Valhalla to Odin and the Aesir (Germanic peoples), and so on.

However, if one takes it exactly, one can say only certainly that the souls have no more their bodies after death. The motive of the hereafter as a place serves only the figurative orientation.

The soul in the body of a living person and the soul of a dead person are not in two different places – the only difference is that in one case the soul has a body and in the other case it does not. Therefore, when a living person travels to his own soul, he travels, so to speak, to the beyond.

For this reason also the journey of a shaman into the beyond is ultimately only a figurative paraphrase for the fact that he or she travels to a soul, i.e. makes contact with it. The same is true for ancestor worship and meditations. For this reason, the Tibetan Book of the Dead is at the same time a guide for the afterlife journey, on which the shaman accompanies the dying, and for meditation, with the help of which the yogi finds his own soul, among other things.

Thus, the afterlife, where the devil dwells, is not a real place at all, but only the "disembodied state" of the soul.

17

It is interesting that here also an error appears as one of the roots of the devil – Buddha described hatred, greed and error as the three basic evils in life and the devil is the basic evil in the monotheistic religions, i.e. especially in Judaism, Christianity and Islam.

Error is one of the roots of the devil – what about hatred and greed? They can also be found quite easily …

The normal state of man is self-expression, i.e. a radiance. When this radiance meets an obstacle, this ray becomes stronger to remove the obstacle: effort. However, if the obstacle does not give way, there are first of all two ways of reaction:

> 1. One gives up. As a result, the radiance, the power, the life-force begins to turn in circles – this is experienced as grief. Grief is a cycle of wishing, hoping, trying, failing, wishing, hoping, etc.
>
> Finally, this circular movement in the psyche becomes faster and faster and its circles become narrower and narrower until the movement finally breaks down and becomes point-like – this is then depression.
>
> 2. One increases the radiance and the striving more and more – this is experienced as anger. The pressure of one's life force against the obstacle increases.
>
> When one experiences the issue as existential, one eventually becomes single-minded in one's striving to remove the obstacle. Through this fixation on the removal of an obstacle, anger eventually becomes hatred.

Through what can one get into such a fixation? Ultimately, this always happens when it is based on an existential feeling without any flexibility. Probably the most important existential feeling of this kind is fear, which is thus the main origin of hate.

Since the devil as evil is what one wants to avoid at all costs, the devil is also what one hates.

The horned one has therefore at least already two roots: error as well as hate, which is based on the fear of death.

The fear of death as a root of the devil is also shown in the fact that his herd-animal-form was created by the ideas about the reprocreation.

This leaves greed as the third possible root of the devil – according to Buddha. It can easily be found in the seven deadly sins to which the devil wants to seduce people in Christianity: envy (Moon), avarice (Mercury), lust (Venus), pride (Sun), anger (Mars), gluttony (Jupiter) and laziness (Saturn).

Actually envy and avarice/greed belong together to the Moon – the deadly sin of Mercury should actually be something like errors, conceit, bossiness and the like.

But in any case, as correspondence to greed in Buddha's world view, envy, greed and avarice are to be found here.

The seven deadly sins can be compared to Buddha's three evils:

- error: arrogance, haughtiness
- hatred: anger
- greed: envy, greed, lust, gluttony, laziness

The three evils are also closely related to the first three phases of human development:

- In the <u>oral phase</u> (0-1 year), the baby lives in symbiosis with its mother. Ideally, it is provided with everything it needs during this time – it then experiences an abundance of warmth, nourishment, affection, and so on. Ideally, this results in a comprehensive "yes" to everything – security.

However, if instead the baby experiences lack, it either becomes increasingly noisy, resulting in the attitude of the addict (greed), or increasingly quiet, resulting in the attitude of the ascetic (repressed greed).

- In the <u>anal stage</u> (1-3 years), the toddler becomes more independent and learns to talk and walk. Ideally, during this time, it learns about its own power and can develop an inner clarity about what is good for it and what is not. This ideally results in a clear and powerful "No!" to everything that is not good for him – strength.

However, if the toddler experiences powerlessness and contradictions instead, fear, despair and hatred develop – this either makes him louder and louder, creating the attitude of the perpetrator (power), or quieter and quieter, creating the attitude of the victim (powerlessness).

- In the <u>phallic phase</u> (3-12 years), the child discovers itself as an independent being capable of acting. If all goes well, it can express itself largely unhindered during this time, resulting in a radiant self-love. This is ideally an unwavering "I!!!" at the center of one's life.

However, if instead the child experiences constant obstruction of self-expression, self-doubt arises and the child either becomes louder and louder, creating the attitude of the star (delusions of grandeur), or quieter and quieter, creating the attitude of the fan (inferiority complexes).

The three evils that Buddha identified as the roots of all suffering correspond to the possible problems that can arise in these three phases of human development:

- oral phase   = the greed of the addict and the ascetic
- anal phase   = the hatred of the abuser and the victim
- phallic phase = the error of the star and the fan

In this assignment, the error would be the self-doubt that star and fan carry inside themself – lack of self-knowledge.

A very simple connection between death and the devil can still be recognized: The devil dwells in the afterlife and tries to catch and torture as many souls of the dead as possible.

Here, too, one can observe a development: in the Neolithic period, people lived together with their ancestors – the skulls of the dead were placed in a niche in the dwelling house so that one could contact them at any time via their skulls. The same function is found with the statues of the dead in Egypt, the ancestral shrines in China, the cult of the dead of primitive peoples, etc. People feared death, but not the dead. Therefore, the devil once played a much smaller role – his terror is fed to a large extent by the fear of death and only secondarily by the fear of the dead.

But today Necromancy does not have a good reputation … even the dreaded "Black Riders" in "The Lord of the Rings" are the spirits of deceased kings who have been summoned by Sauron and have to serve him.

3rd Dream Journey to the Devil

"My question to you now, devil, is whether I have correctly identified the three evils or the seven deadly sins as the roots of your being."

"You call 'evil' what you fear – the lack, the attack on you, the lie and the destruction of your radiant center. What else are you asking me?"

"Hm ... I always have doubts whether I have already grasped all aspects with my thinking – people are naturally one-sided in their cognition and thinking, because everyone wears his own horoscope as 'glasses' and as 'blinders', but of course also uses it as a 'microscope' and as a 'telescope'. In what respect am I one-sided?"

"You are too focused on understanding. You don't use your power to the same degree. You have a completely dented egoism."

"O.k. ... I can agree with that. And what do you recommend there?"

"Face your fear. Do what your kundalini advised you to do: 'look, feel, embrace': That's the way to integrate and heal something – look at what's there; feel the power in it; embrace what's split off back into you."

"My dented egoism is my personal devil, so to speak?"
"Yes – and that is the only devil you should take care of first."
"Hm ... yes ... thank you, devil ... ... Ho!"

4.   Hell

The devil, as is generally known, lives in hell. Why, actually? "Hell" means "cave." But why does he live in a cave?

In order to be able to recognize this, one must go back again rather far in the history of humanity.

At least 1.7 million years ago, the first huts were built by the distant ancestors of today's humans. From them wall circles from piled up stones remained preserved, which were covered presumably by a vault of branches, hides, leaves and so on.

Of course there were other "huts" before, like the burrow of the fox, the nest of the birds, the goblet of the squirrel, the castle of the beaver etc., but these stone circle huts of the Stone Age people were the first "stone buildings".

Even earlier we can find the eggs of the reptiles, which were also a "shelter". It is likely that the first huts of humans were also associated with the mother's womb, that is, with the memory of the time before birth – both were the only interior spaces known at that time.

Then, 600,000 years ago, these huts became much more important in Eurasia at the beginning of the Ice Age, as it was almost impossible to survive without them in the cold of that time.

These huts were also heated from the beginning of the Ice Age: for this purpose, stones were heated in a fire in front of the hut and then carried into the hut on the shoulder blade bone of a deer or similar, and then the entrance was closed again. With the help of heated stones it was also possible to cook meat and vegetable soups in a hide bag at that time.

In those days, when there were no schools, no teaching and no social security, parents were the greatest source of advice and help in one's life. Therefore, people tried to keep in touch with them even after their death. This task was taken over by the shamans.

One became a shaman by experiencing an astral journey during a near-death and then successfully practicing to be able to repeat this astral journey at will. During an astral journey, one experiences floating above one's own physical body, flying to different places and being able to perceive everything there. This was the origin of the ideas about the existence of a soul.

This first "religious principle" was depicted with the help of a bird on a stick – this motif can already be found in the late Paleolithic period about 25,000 years ago in the cave of Lascaux next to a wounded or dead hunter. From this bird-staff the totem poles were already developed in the late Old Stone Age, which represent above all the body of a human being (tree trunk) with his soul-bird on his shoulders. There are differentiated stone forms of them already around 10,000 BC, which shows that there must have been a longer tradition of wooden totem poles before that.

Since both the hut heated with glowing stones and the ancestors gave security and safety, the Paleopithic people will have associated both with each other – especially since both also fitted extremely well to the association of the hut with the belly of the pregnant mother. Therefore, the ancestors were preferably invoked in the heated hut – thus the sweat lodge developed as the earliest form of the temple.

Since the ancestors gave their descendants security and support in the sweat lodge, it was obvious to associate the poles, from which the framework of the sweat lodge was built, with the ancestors. This symbolism can still be found today in sweat lodge ceremonies. The sweat lodge poles were very simple bird poles or totem poles, so to speak.

Because of the symbolism of rebirth, it is possible that a simplified sweat lodge in the form of a brushwood mound was erected over a grave in the Old Stone Age – the hut or brushwood mound was the belly of the earth pregnant with the dead. Such brushwood mounds are still found in historical times among the Scythians in the ritual of their sungod-godfather Papaios, in which very likely his evening death and his morning rebirth were represented.

At the beginning of the Neolithic period (10,000 BC), the pregnancy belly symbolism of the sweat lodge was depicted in much greater detail than before at Göbekli Tepe in northern Mesopotamia and other sites nearby:

- a circular wall with a domed roof of branches and skins = the belly of the Great Mother

- a slightly smaller circular wall with a dome roof of branches and skins inside the previous stone circle = the child in the belly of the Great Mother – the ritual participants sat there

- a covered passage leading to the larger circle = the vagina of the Great Mother

- a stone slab with a big hole at the beginning of this passage, through which one crawled into the passage and then further into the inner circle = the pudency of the Great Mother

- a short connecting wall from the outer to the inner circle = the umbilical cord between mother and child

- two panthers on the entrance stone slab = the two panthers of the Mother Goddess, symbolizing her power, which she was asked for by the hunters of that time

   - eight T-shaped pillars in the inner wall = the ancestors protecting the ritual participants (the former staffs of the sweat lodge; „8“ was the number of completeness in the binary number system of that time)

   - two big T-pillars in the center of the inner circle = the archetypes of the body and the soul

When the shamans traveled to a concrete ancestor, they did it on his grave. This has led to the fact that the shamans have generally sat on a symbolic grave when they have made an afterlife journey. This grave symbol can be a brushwood mound (Scythians), a seat base made of twigs (Celts), a flat pedestal (Harappa), a flat table (Egyptians), a small or large pedestal (Germanic tribes), a lotus flower (Indians), and so on.

One of the names of the Great Mother of the time of the builders of the temples of Göbekli Tepe has been "Aset", i.e. "the sitting on". From this name has been derived a lot of later godesses names like "Isis" and "Astarte". She is "the goddess, who sits on the bench in the temple", "the goddess who sits on her throne", "the godess who sits on the tempel" and "the goddess who sits on the burial mound".

Images of a man (probably a shaman) or woman (probably the goddess) standing a tempel are already known from the early Neolithic.

The mound is a sweat lodge or a brushwood mound built of earth and stones. Like the temples of Göbekli Tepe, it consists of a passage leading to a chamber in the center – the vagina and belly of the Great Mother, who was probably conceived here as the earth goddess.

The megalithic complexes have the same structure as the temples of Göbekli Tepe – they are only larger and have no walls:

   - inner circular wall (child) → inner circle of menhirs

   - outer circle wall (belly) → outer circle of menhirs

   - connecting wall (umbilical cord) → missing

   - passage (vagina) → menhir avenue leading to the menhir circle

   - two panther statuettes at the entrance → two big menhirs at the beginning of the menhir avenue

   - eight T-pillars in the inner wall → the inner circle of tall menhirs

   - two big T-pillars in the center of the inner circle → the two big menhirs in the center of the menhir circle

Most temples from the Neolithic period to the present day consist of a passageway leading to a center, which is usually a chamber containing the statue of one or more deities. This corresponds to the corridor and circle of the sweat lodges with their "igloo ground plan". Often this type of temple has at its entrance two high towers or entrance pillars (steeples) corresponding to the two panthers of the Great Mother. Sometimes these two panthers or lions also stand as large statues in front of the entrance of the temple.

The mandala temples, which are mostly dedicated to the Sun God, have omitted the aisle and consist only of the circle. In this circle, however, the cardinal point symbolism, which can already be found in the temples of Göbekli Tepe in a very pronounced way, is often represented quite clearly: four points on the outside, in the center of which is the sun.

The tower of Jericho, which dates from the early Neolithic (9000 BC) and is oriented to the course of the sun, and also the towers of Çatal Höyük (7000 BC), from which the goddess of the afterlife in the form of a vulture fetched the dead, represent, like the world tree, the umbilical cord between this world (earth) and the afterlife (heaven). Therefore, in this context, the goddess of the afterlife and the sun mother appears not as an earth goddess, but as a vulture goddess: the mother of the soul birds is also a bird – the largest bird. She is later known in Egypt as the goddess Mut, i.e. "mother".

The pyramid is a large mound tomb built entirely of stone, which, because of its four sides, also incorporates the symbolism of the mandala temple. The passage is found in two ways: first as the passage from the Valley Temple to the pyramid and second as the passage that leads to the interior of the pyramid. The great height of the pyramids corresponds to the sky ladder symbolism of the tower temples.

The burial chamber in the tumuli has become the model for the "hell" where the devil dwells. The word "hell" is a variant of the German word "Höhle" (cave) and the northern Germanic word "Hel" (hel), which was used to refer to a cave and to the cave underworld and to the goddess of the afterlife.

The devil, as a goat-man or more generally as a herd-animal man, is the dead man in such a tumulus burial chamber. Thus, the devil was originally the dead man in his burial chamber.

There were different variants of burials in the barrows. One of them is the cremation burial. In it, the dead person was cremated on a chariot or on a ship – both of which served as a vehicle to the afterlife. Then the ashes of the burial fire were covered with earth and stones, so that a mound was formed.

The cremation burial has a longer history. It was obvious to invite the ancestors also at the common meal of the clan and to hand them symbolically a few pieces of meat.

From this the offerings to the ancestors developed. In order to be able to send these offerings to the afterlife, the offerings of course had to "die" – so these offerings were broken, burned, sunk in a lake or otherwise destroyed or made inaccessible. Burning in a fire was one of the simplest and sensually most impressive variants of sending something to the underworld.

The burning of the offerings gave rise to the motif of fire as the gateway to the afterlife – this is the root of the lighting of a fire or candle as the opening of a ritual and also of the "eternal fires" in some temples as well as the great fire in the temple at the Mysteries of Eleusis. All these fires open the gate to the other world, so that the contact to the ancestors and to the gods becomes possible.

Also the firewalking, known among others by the Germanic, Celts and Greeks, originally had the symbolism of an afterlife journey – if you walk barefoot over the embers, you go to the afterlife.

The various types of trial by fire, such as putting one's hand in the fire or holding one's hand in boiling oil, were also such afterlife journeys: the respective god protected the one who spoke the truth from being burned.

With the Indians this fire became even a god in itself: the god Agni in the Rig Veda, who starts every ritual.

It was obvious to open the gate to the afterlife by a fire also at burials and consequently to burn the dead.

This was of course a "mythological circle conclusion": the offerings had to be "killed" by fire, so that they reached the hereafter – consequently also the dead had to be burned, so that they reached the hereafter … although they were already dead …

Especially among the Germanic peoples, the custom of the cremation mound grave has given rise to the idea that a fire continues to burn inside a mound grave – as long as the spirit of the dead buried in this mound grave still remains in this grave.

This burial fire in the barrow then became associated with the burial chamber in the barrow in very late times to form a fire cave – the fire hell of the devil.

The dead were perceived as snakes already in the early Neolithic period in Göbekli Tepe, because both the dead and the snakes resided in the earth (snakes in caves and earth crevices).

Through the connection of the ancestor-snake with the soul-bird the winged snake, i.e. the dragon, was created.

When it was also associated with the funeral fire, it became the fire-breathing winged dragon.

In some countries, especially in China, he was also associated with the lion of strength (mouth, mane, paws) and the fish as a symbol of the soul in the water underworld (barbels on the mouth).

In this way, the devil was also associated with the serpent – where the serpent was reinterpreted from the figure of the dead to the serpent as the cause of death.

The same fate befell the otherworld goddess – she became the feared otherworld goddesses like Hel, Kali or Morrigan and finally "the devil's grandmother". Actually, she should have become "the devil's mother" because of the rebirth symbolism, but since the mother had been so firmly associated with protection and security, the Christian missionaries had to resort to the motif of the devil's grandmother.

When a motif is distorted and thus also polarized, the result is, on the one hand, a horror image that becomes part of the devil's image (in this case "the devils grandmother") and, on the other hand, an ideal image that everyone longed for.

This polarization began with the fact that the beyond-goddess broke down into the longed-for reprocreation-lover and into her dreaded function as afterlife-mistress. The motive of the rebreastfeeding developed relatively neutrally to the ritual potion and furtheron finally to the elixir of life.

While the afterlife mistress was depicted more and more horribly, the reprocreation-lover was painted in more and more brilliant colors. The dead man, including the sungod in the afterlife, who originally as a dead man was distinctly passive, became more and more active in accordance with the medieval conception of man and woman and finally became the hero who went into the cave (burial chamber) to free the virgin (goddess of the afterlife) and to marry her. Since in the cave there was also the dead man as a snake or dragon, the hero valiantly killed the dragon and saved the virgin – a very thorough twisting of the original myth, through which the dragon became another image of evil that had to be destroyed …

To complete the picture, the hell of the devil was also completed by a watchdog, the "hound of hell": Garm among the Teutons, Cerberus among the Greeks, Anubis among the Egyptians, and so on.

This dog had been formerly the guardian of the houses, the companion of the hunters and the sniffer dog of the shamans who help him looking for the way into the beyond.

In the course of the missionization the fire and the trial by fire as an element of the pagan faith was finally reinterpreted to the punishment of burning witches. The clerics "proved" by burning the witches, among other things, that the pagan gods did not help the witches – which, according to the trial by fire, they were supposed to do.

The witch burnings added yet another gruesome aspect to the hellfire motif …

If one looks at this development, it becomes clear that hell had been the pregnant belly of the earth goddess in the beginning – that is, the source of all life … and that this cave had become the origin of death in the end.

This reinterpretation of a help on the afterlife journey and in the afterlife itself to a cause of death is very common in the development of myths. This reinterpretation is always found when there has been a major cultural upheaval – especially when the representatives of a monotheistic religion have sought to eradicate another, older religion.

4th Dream Journey to the Devil

This time I do not have a conversation with the devil ("acoustic dream journey"), but travel into the world of images ("optical dream journey"): I take a closer look at hell. What I will find is still quite unclear to me ...

It's dusk – evening, not yet night ... there's a path in a narrow valley, which, however, has no steep slopes ... I go slightly downhill, but on the valley bottom, strangely enough, there's no stream or something, although the valley would actually be big enough for that ...

The valley ends at a steeper slope – there is a cave entrance ... I would have expected the entrance to a burial mound, but this is a natural cave – at least the entrance looks like one ...

I go in ... rocky ground, small stones, hardly any sand, rather a little gravel, but edged pebbles, no round river pebbles – this is unusual for such a cave ... I go further in, it leads slightly downwards ... the passage meanders a little, but it is almost always the same in size ...

I feel that there have been people in here a long time ago ... the passage becomes larger, the ceiling partly higher, the whole thing no longer seems like a tube, but clearly more angular ... I can feel that there are cave paintings somewhere here ... now I come into a larger hall ... on the left in front there is a life-size bear modeled out of clay (I know this bear from my archeologial studies) ... there are also some bear skulls ... there are half-burned bones, which were used as torches in the caves in the Paleolithic Age ...

On the far left is a shallow, narrow cave in which one could just lie – its floor is completely cleared of stones and the like ... is this a ritual cave where rebirth was depicted?

At the back right, a passage continues to an underground lake – but I'm not going there ...

Where are the cave paintings? ... In the back on the left I see one up on the ceiling – they must have used ladders or racks back then ... there are bison and reindeer ... and water waves, some fish – the ancestors in the water underworld?

"Where is the most important thing to find here?"

I'm drawn to the back left ... I go there ....

There is a cleared space, it is largely smooth – no larger stones ... it is about 6m in diameter or maybe a bit more – I can't estimate that accurately ... well, more like 7m ... there are stones all around – to sit on?, as a boundary?, or both?

"Is this the most important place in this cave?"

"Yes, this is the ritual place."

"Who is answering me here?"

"Me."

I see a man coming from the right, wearing a bearskin – so he must be a shaman.

"Are you a shaman?"

"Yes."

"What is the most important thing I can find here? And what did you use this place for? I know such places in caves from archaeological research reports ..."

"The most important thing is you."

"I can find myself here?"

"Your soul."

"Because this is the underworld? The soul realm?"

"Yes."

"And what were you doing here – 25,000 years ago or so?"

"We traveled to the underworld to the souls – to the souls of our ancestors and to our own souls."

The caves with the paintings, clay statuettes, and ritual sites from the late Paleo-lithic period obviously symbolically correspond to the sweat lodges and later temples and burial mounds: the womb of the Great Mother.

"Is that right, what I just wrote here?"

"Yes."

"Can you show me some of what you did in those underground ritual places back then?"

"Yes – that's why you're here now. That's why you came here. And that's why I've been waiting for you."

"Yes ... well ... is there anything you want me to do?"

"Sit here on one of the stones at the edge of the circle."

I see someone approaching me – from the entrance to this underground stone circle, the stone on the right front ... that's the place where I also sit when I conduct sweat lodges ...

"Does the place have any significance?"

"It is your place. Be quiet now."

"O.k. ..."

He sits to my left, where the entrance is, and faces the center. I wait ... ... it's

29

getting warmer – funny ... why, actually? ... It is life force, not physical warmth ... there is a very similar feeling here as in a sweat lodge ... the cave starts to feel organic – this is also like in the sweat lodge ...

The shaman starts calling animal spirits – I can see them vaguely all around the circle ... bison, reindeer ... it's all herd animals coming, I think ... so this is not a normal sweat lodge ceremony, where you call the serpent, the bear, the eagle and the buffalo – here are different animals ... this feels like security here ....

I actually expect the spirits of people to come here, but so far I don't see anyone ...

"Silence – even inside."

"Yes, alright ..."

The shaman takes red ocher and begins to paint me – I know this also from excavation reports and from primitive peoples and from early Egypt ... oh yes – also silent inwardly ... There are longitudinal strokes with five fingers at a time – so the classic pattern of body painting known for example from Africa ... this is invigorating, strengthening ...

I suddenly notice that around the stone circle some bone torches are burning ... they soot pleasantly little ... The shaman rubs some of his saliva on my thymus-intermediate chakra at the upper end of my breastbone ... Is something supposed to open there? ... Strangely enough, it's more like a connection ... um – am I being affiliated here right now?

"Silence and look!"

I can feel the connections ... to the animals around the stone circle and also to some people I can see by now, who have sat down in the circle – many children, some women, few men ... they are very unselfconscious, they feel comfortable here, they are very relaxed – also the children ... they watch ...

The shaman bends my head a little bit forward, my chin towards my chest ... he puts a fur hat with two bison horns on it ... this transforms me, I feel different ... how should I put it ... more alive, more fulfilled, more organic, more integrated ... somehow more right and more alive ... and I clearly feel part of a community ... a community of living and dead, a community of souls ...

The people in the stone circle begin to softly clap their thighs rhythmically ... are they humming? I'm not sure ... I suddenly feel warmth, closeness, touch all over my body, even if no one touches me ... this is the kind of touch that one has as an unborn child in the womb – no breathing, no eating, always warm and weightless ... this is real security ...

It's like a sweat lodge ceremony with no sweat lodge and no sweating ... that feels good ... letting go of all tension and becoming an unborn in the womb again ....

I just stay there for a while in this state ... ... that feels good ... ... the others also experience the same ... they are also in this security ... ...

... ...

... ...
... ...

"Stay in this security when you leave the cave again – do not leave this security ... it is what nourishes you and what bears you ..."

"Yes ... I will do that ... Thank you very, very much!"

... ...
... ...
... ...

Finally, I say goodbye with a smile, which is returned to me by all, and I go outside again ... and I stay at the same time in this security, as the shaman has told me ...

So this is what the "hell" has originally once been ... we have really lost our way quite badly in the course of our religious history ...

5. The Evil Serpent

The snake has been a symbol for the soul of the dead buried in the earth already in the late Paleolithic – maybe this symbolism is even older. In any case, it already appears on the stone pillars in the temples of Göbekli Tepe 12,000 years ago in northern Mesopotamia.

Since this symbolism had already fanned out into several other symbolisms 12,000 years ago, it can be assumed that the motif of the serpent ancestors had already existed for a long time at the beginning of the Neolithic period – that is, at least already in the late Paleolithic period (50,000 – 10,000 BC).

From the snake as an ancestor spirit living in the earth (the dead in the graves, the snakes in crevices and caves), the snake has become a symbol for the afterlife.

The second derived symbolism is the snake as that which comes from the afterlife: the blessing of the ancestors for their descendants.

The third derived symbolism of the snake is the kundalini, i.e. the life force rising in the body, which has apparently been compared to the blessing of the ancestors rising from the earth. In medition the Kundalini fire actually rises out of the earth into the root chakra and then further up to the crown chakra. The Kundalini has been known to the shamans from very early times, which is simply because the learning of astral travel (the central skill of a shaman) and the awakening of the Kundalini fire largely coincide: In both cases, one learns first and foremost to become aware of one's own life force body.

Because of the double association of the snake with death, on the one hand through its poison and on the other hand through the fact that it has been a symbol for the ancestors, the snake has been linked in a particularly intense way with death and therefore also with the fear of death. This brought it close to the figure of the devil, who is, among other things, the embodiment of fears.

There was another important development in snake symbolism in the middle of the Neolithic period:

Around 10,500 BC, the last Ice Age ended, and with it the Old Stone Age. The first temples were built in Göbekli Tepe, people were able to live together in larger groups because of the significantly greater abundance of game in the warmer climate, and agriculture was invented around 8500 BC – thus began the Neolithic period, which ended with the founding of the Egyptian Empire around about 3150 BC.

While there had been quite heavy snowfalls during the Ice Age and quite heavy rains during the early Neolithic, it became much drier from 6000 BC onwards. As a result, farming became more difficult – which was especially true of the southern

Russian steppe, where the ancestors of the later Indo-Europeans, who had migrated there from Mesopotamia around 7000 BC, had farmed at the time.

Since this drought was a big problem and forced the people in this country, which gradually became a steppe, to change from agriculture to semi-nomadic cattle breeding, they naturally wondered where the rain had gone.

In the conceptions of that time there was a big fresh water sea under the earth – the Sumerians called it in later times "Abzu". This motive was due to the fact that the fresh water of the springs bubbles up from the earth and also the clouds on the horizon seem to rise out of the earth. Because of this freshwater sea under the earth, the image of the water underworld, in which the dead were, was also created – possibly there was an association with the amniotic fluid in the womb of a mother.

Obviously, the drought arose because someone prevented the rain from rising from the underworld and watering the earth. But who could that be? This someone had to be very great – but it could not be the Otherworld Goddess, since she was benevolent to humans.

However, there was a second great being in the underworld, to whom such a rain robbery could fit: By the fact that the serpent was conceived as a figure of the ancestral spirits, it had also become a symbol of the way into the underworld and the way out of it again. Also the sun died in the evening and sank far in the west in the sea or in the earth, then traveled through the entire underworld and was reborn in the morning in the east. So the sun's path through the underworld was a serpent that reached from the western horizon to the eastern horizon – a mighty serpent!

This snake way of the sun through the underworld is also described in some variants of the Egyptian Book of the Dead. Also the Midgard snake of the Teutons or the snake-shaped goddess Tiamat of the Sumerians are pictures of this giant snake in the underworld.

Apparently it was this giant snake that kept the rain in the underworld. It obviously stole it every year in spring anew. As the autumn thunderstorms show, however, at the end of summer the god of heaven and thunder succeeded in defeating this giant serpent and freeing the rain again – the thunderstorms are the noise of the battle of the god of heaven against the giant serpent.

From this motive the many different dragon and snake fights have arisen from Thor's quarrel with the giant snake Jörmungandr in the water underworld to the fight of the archangel Michael with the dragon. This motif has also been added to the story of the hero who frees the fair maiden from the clutches of the dragon in his cave – this cave dragon has essentially been a reinterpretation of the dead (hero) in serpent form at his reincarnation with the otherworld goddess in the burial chamber of his barrow.

Again, there has been a hardship, i.e. the drought, which caused a lot of trouble to the arable farmers from 6000 BC on, which has been the occasion to design an "evil figure" – the devil obviously consists of everything that people fear.

One of the best known "evil serpents" is certainly the serpent in paradise in the creation story in the Bible. There, the goddess as the rebirth mother of the serpent ancestral spirits has become the seductress Eve …

5th Dream Journey to the Devil

"Would you like to tell me something else about your serpent form, devil?"
"Why should I?"
"Do you care at all about people understanding who you are?"
"You should care yourselves about understanding me."
"So it makes no difference to you how people see you?"
"It has an effect on me, but I have no preferences there."
"Hm … that's a perspective from which I've never looked at it … Does the devil or do the gods have preferences? … I suppose that they are simply what they are and that they simply express what they are?"
"Yes."
"And that they can also change and then just express this changed state?"
"Yes."
"And if we understand you, could that lead us to fear you less, and especially to fear fewer things in the world and in our lives, and thus to carry a smaller 'personal devil' within us?"
"You could put it that way – if you look as a healer. But do you really think you can erase all pain in the world? All violence? All fear? All greed? All error? All suffering? Do you think you are Buddha?"
"Hm … So you are not just a figure that has been created over the millennia by errors, fears and greed, and that can be healed, for example, by clearing up the errors and reintegrating feelings? Are you something like the eternal struggle of people against the world?"
"You're getting closer to the point …"
"But this sounds very Scorpionic – this fundamental contradiction between ego and world, between will and destiny … but you really seem to be a Scorpionic figure, so 'Scorpion' in the astrological sense …
Are you simply the obstacles, the endless confrontation of man with the world?"
"Not badly formulated …"
"But the Scorpion view is only one of many possible views … the views of the other

eleven signs of the zodiac lead to other world views ..."

"But all know suffering and therefore know the devil!"

"There you emphasize now again in a Scorpionic way the failure, the resistances, the pain, the fear, the greed, the lack, the powerlessness, the self-doubts and so on. ..."

"They are the central experience."

"For a Scorpio."

"Who could perceive any other feeling as more intense than pain?"

"You put the most intense in the center and make it the measure of all things."

"What else would make sense?"

"Putting the most frequent thing in the center? The pleasant? The identity? The self-expression? The dance of life? The enjoyment? The curiosity? The cognition?"

"I want to see how you come to realizations when you are in intense pain! Or how you express yourself when you suffer!"

"I can certainly do that ... but I can already see that we can't agree on this point ..."

"That's because the contradiction is the essence."

"Which again confirms that we can't agree. ... But I don't need that in this case either – after all, first of all I just want to understand who you are ... and with that I'm gradually making progress.

Thank you very much!"

The devil just grumbles to himself ...

"Ho!"

Also Buddha put pain and the end of pain in the center of his world view – was he a Scorpio, too? It would fit to much of his teachings …

6. God and Devil

In the Paleolithic Age, direct contact has been the important element – the experience, the presence, the quick reaction, the perception. In that time it was enough to process things in the simplest way, i.e. by associations. This is still the fundamental basis of brain activity today.

The "good state" was abundance, security, warmth, food … thus the (Great) Mother … These qualities were expressed by the sweat lodge.

The "evil" was simply that which was unpleasant: hunger, pain, lack, cold, death of a human being, etc.

In the Neolithic period, 500 times more people lived together, different professions emerged, the first villages, agriculture, animal husbandry – life became so complex that it was no longer possible to know everyone and to know everything. Therefore, the comparison arose as a processing principle: the parable, the analogy, the myths, the cult, the tradition – and as essence of this attitude the rightness.

This rightness is the right sowing date, the straight axis of the potter's wheel, the roundness of the wheel, the right tuning of the harp, and so on. The word for this correctness has been the central concept in these worldviews:

- the ma'at ("mother") of the Egyptians,
- the me ("mother") of the Sumerians,
- the ho'zhong ("beauty") of the Navahos,
- the tashi ("happy destiny") of the Tibetans,
- the tao ("way") of the Chinese,
- the sidr ("ancient way") of the Teutons,
- the rita ("wheel") of the Indians,
- the asha ("wheel") of the Persians,
- the aya ("wheel") of the Hittites,
- the ritus ("wheel") of the Romans,
- the dharma ("verse measure") of the Indians,
- the fhirinne ("truth") of the Celts,
- the pravda ("truth") of the Slavs,
- the dikaios ("justice") of the Greeks,
  etc.

Deviation from this rightness caused suffering and failure and was therefore something to be avoided. The "non-righteousness" was rarely formulated and named as an independent principle. It is found, for example, among the Egyptians as "isfet" and among the Hopis as "koyaanisqatsi". Sometimes, but rather rarely, these principles have been conceived of as goddesses – for example, both the Ma'at and the Isfet of the Egyptians are goddesses. Here the origin of the rightness is still recognizable as a derivation of the security with the Great Mother.

The "non-rightness" in this epoch is one of the precursors of the devil.

With the foundation of the Egyptian empire around approx. 3150 BC, with which also kingship in general was founded, a new principle of order arose. By the king a very large area was steered centrally. For this a number system, a writing, an administration etc. were necessary. The great advantage of this system was that through the large-scale coordination of, among other things, agriculture, including irrigation, a much more secure supply of food could be achieved.

In this system, the rightness of the Neolithic period evolved into the command of the king – the will of the king directs the whole.

This new principle of centralism also had effects on religion: In the circle of the many gods, the sun god or the primeval god came to the fore, eventually becoming the father of the gods, who evolved into the one god having different aspects, which then finally led to monotheism. Man shaped his gods according to the model of his own culture.

The king was now the sustainer of rightness and justice – and he was the representative of the One God on earth, whereby the One God was ultimately the actual sustainer of rightness and justice.

But there was an obvious contradiction: if God was just and if he was almighty, why does he allow so much injustice on earth? And why does he not even punish it? The solution to this problem was the court of the hereafter: there one received the "just punishment" for one's wrongdoing in this world.

This punishment, of course, was soon illustrated in increasingly drastic ways: for example, in Egypt, the dead person who failed the afterlife court was eaten by the monster Ammut, who was a hippopotamus with a crocodile head and panther front legs. Here we find again the connection of the devil (monster) with death (annihilation of the soul).

So the devil-monster was in the beginning a helper of the one just God, through which he punishes those who did not follow the rightness or the law of the king in their life. The devil was originally God's executioner …

However, this monster soon took on a life of his own and eventually became an adversary of God. He became the "anti-power" to God's omnipotence, which should explain the suffering and injustice in the world. In the monotheistic religions, however, it was never explained conclusively why God created the devil – after all, he created everything. Neither was it explained why, if God created the devil, he gave people the freedom to choose between God and the devil – and then punished people if they chose the devil, i.e. "evil". Why did God give people freedom if he then punishes them when they use their freedom?

The monotheistic system is not conclusive if it does not contain the motive of the devil. This is due to the fact that in every centralistic system there is an all-controlling will, but of course there are always people who want and do something else. But the real problem is that God is seen as a king. A king is powerful, but not omnipotent – therefore there are of course injustices in his kingdom … that is quite normal. But if God is understood as all-powerful and all-just, and perhaps also as all-wise, then one gets a problem with the interpretation of injustice in the world …

One could also say quite simply that the idea of a God who is just in an earthly way is an illusion – a transfer of earthly conditions to the hereafter. The same kind of error had already originated with the reprocreation, with the hereafter and with the hell.

6th Dream Journey to the Devil

"I suppose that during the kingship you acquired a much greater hardness, devil – is that true? The power of kingship and the demand of obedience by the king to his subjects should have given the same power intensity to all deviations from the king's orders and all contradictions to them ... and of course even more to the deviations from 'God's law', so in Christianity e.g. from the ten commandments."

"Finished talking?! Stop babbling when you ask a question and listen to the answer before you ask the next question!"

"O.K."

"Yeah, right."

"Um ... is there anything else you'd like to say about that?"

"During the Paleolithic Age, there was definitely suffering, but no devil. Also in the Neolithic period there was no devil, but only the non-righteousness, which has been personified sometimes, but only very rarely and also only at the transition to king-ship. I became an independent figure only in kingship."

"In this epoch very many principles have been personified ...

... ...

Have I overlooked something else that contributed to your development in this epoch? What has been important for your biography and your being?"

"The perpetrator's fear of the one of his victims who will eventually attack him."

"Um – because the rulers are always afraid of the revolt of the ruled? At least when they are despots ..."

"Yes – this also made the devil a being who wields power, who is the 'Dark Ruler' that the 'Light Ruler' fears ..."

"That's a problem then, when the ruler identifies with his position of power and defends it against everything, isn't it?"

"Yes."

"If the ruler has the welfare of the whole people in mind, that's different, I suppose?"

"Yes."

"Then, yes, 'Sauron' in 'Lord of the Rings' and 'Lord Voldemort' in the 'Harry Potter' books, among others, are also character studies of the devil! ..."

"No – Sauron and Voldemort have many of the characteristics of the Devil, but they are a concrete demigod and a human, respectively. This gives them a slightly different dynamic. Voldemort, for example, wants immortality – I don't need to seek that, since I will live as long as you humans are still afraid of fear and suffering and live in error."

"Does that mean that the Dementors in the 'Harry Potter' books are even closer to the devil, right?"

"No – they are the shadow of an individual, that is, what he fears."

"Um ... and the 'Black Riders' in 'Lord of the Rings'?"

"They are the spirits of dead kings, i.e. they illustrate above all the fear of death by which the dead appear as threatening."

"You portray this very precisely, strikingly, and insightfully – these conversations with you are downright beneficial, devil. I would not have thought a year ago that I would ever write such a sentence."

"Merci."

"Is there anything else you could tell me about the devil in the era of kingship and monotheism?"

"The 'infernal hierarchies' are a parallel formation to the hierarchies in the church and kingdoms. They are the dark equivalent of the light heavenly hosts ... though it is always a question of what you actually want – it depends on which host you find 'light' and which you find 'dark'. It's like in war – one always finds one's army good and the other evil ... consequently, all wars are always fought in the name of good by all sides involved."

"Well, also your epithet 'Prince of Darkness' shows the principle of hierarchy of a kingdom ... also in the classical demon invocations from the Middle Ages, first God, then the archangels, then the angels etc. are invoked to receive protection from them, and then the devils, then the lords of hell and finally Satan as the king of hell himself are invoked ... it must all go its orderly official way, otherwise the whole thing does not work ..."

Oh, the devil grins ... he seems to like my description ....

"Is there anything more you would like to say about this, devil?"

"We should go for a drink together sometime, buddy!"

39

"Er ... I don't like alcohol, but if it's okay with you if I have a sloe-juice, I'd love to!"

"O.k., come on then!"

"Er ... yes ... o.k. ..."

He leads me through the narrow, dark streets of a medieval village, or perhaps rather a small town, to an inn ... I have almost never been in inns ....

It is loud and crowded, warm and quite bright – quite a hustle and bustle ... in the back on the right is a table at which only a single man with a full red beard sits ... There the devil leads me. The two seem to know each other ... The devil calls out the order to the waitress and a woman brings me a glass of sloe juice, the devil something spiritous and rather clear and the red beard a large tankard of mead ...

Where does this dream journey lead to now?

... ...

"Are you Thor, Red Beard? You have a resemblance to him, but you also look very different..."

He laughs ... "No, I'm not him, even if I know him well – just call me 'Barbarossa'."

"'Barbarossa' simply means 'Red Beard' – but you're not the Germanic thunder god Thor and probably not King Friedrich Barbarossa, are you?"

Barbarossa laughs out loud ...

"But who are you, then? And why do we meet you here?"

He just grins ...

"Why did you come here with me, devil?"

"Because it will do you good, Harry."

"Um ... are you Mars? Some Germanic Martian variant, or rather, Mars in Germanic medieval garb?"

"Score!"

"And we meet you here because you are part of my own shadow?"

"Another hit! Good warrior, forsooth!"

"But for being my shadow, I find you distinctly likeable ..."

"Well – everyone who has a shadow – well, just about everyone – fears his shadow, and at the same time he longs for it, for there is nothing whose integration could make him happier."

"Um ... yes ... I haven't had it formulated so clearly until now ..."

"You just don't go to pubs often enough!"

When Barbarossa sees my puzzled face, he starts laughing loudly ...

"Now I understand why you, devil, have led me to this pub to you, Barbarossa. What can you show me or teach me, Barbarossa?"

"Come inside me with your consciousness."

"O.K. ... wait a minute ... ... this feels very carefree, open and direct ... a life with an open visor, so to speak ... and your sword arm and your shield arm are

equally strong ... I fight almost only with my sword arm ..."

"And since you are right-handed and consequently hold your shield with your left, your left shoulder joint has been hurting you for half a year."

"Er ... now I'm flabbergasted ... I haven't come up with this interpretation yet ... in any case, it can't be dismissed out of hand, even if I'm not completely convinced of it yet ..."

Barbarossa laughs at me again ... "But you take everything seriously, you guy! It has something to do with it, but it is not the cause – the cause is your attitude while writing, as you have already noticed. But still, the one with the strained shield arm is a nice picture that makes you understand something, isn't it?"

"So you play with images?"

"Of course ... everyone does, don't they? The politicians who want to convince others of something, the hypnotists who want to lull others, the bosses who want to force obedience, the clerics who want to discipline their flocks, the artists with their images and melodies ..."

"Well ... but there is also precise analogy as in the I Ching, in Astrology, in the Kabbalistic Tree of Life, etc."

"That's something else ... and your head doesn't need expansion right now, but your hara, your belly, your feelings – just your Mars."

"And there all methods are right?"

"If they lead to the goal ... how do you say? 'All is fair in love and war.' and 'Enlightenment doesn't care how you attain it.'"

"Now I have quite deviated from my visit to your consciousness ... ... What else is there? ... Hm, a strong sexual urge – that's also quite carefree ... ... There's also a good nature and a serenity – that reminds me of Hagrid in 'Harry Potter' ... There's also enjoyment ... rather simple pleasures like sex, adventure, eating, drinking, riding, wrestling ... ..."

Hm, I once again return to myself here at this pub table ...

"I suppose that you can show me more, right?"

The two look at each other and grin in agreement ... "Sure thing," they say, "come with me."

They walk with me through a door next to the bar, where quite a few people are talking quite loudly at the moment and are obviously quite drunk already ... It continues through a corridor and then into a larger room, where there are many men and women ... many are unclothed and just having sex with each other ... others are sitting in a corner smoking ... a few others are playing the lute together ... some are also just sleeping or dozing off, still others are drinking ...

"Where are we here, Barbarossa?"

"These are the things that you missed, that you often didn't allow yourself to get or that you did get but didn't tell anyone about ..."

41

"Is that the content of my shadow now, so to speak?"

The devil and Barbarossa just look at me mischievously and remain silent ...

"No, that can't actually be my shadow – that's just the 'gray shadow', not the 'black shadow', i.e. the semi-integrated part of my shadow ... Then there should actually be another door and another corridor back there, leading me to my 'black shadow', shouldn't there?"

"Score!"

"Hm ... that is like in all descriptions of the other world a way through different chambers ... like in the fairy tale 'The Nut Branch' or in Dante's 'Inferno' ... O.k. – I also want to see the next chamber!"

Barbarossa turns to the devil, "Well, at least your buddy you brought there is brave."

I walk to the other side of the room and then through the door ... the corridor beyond is clearly darker than the previous corridor from the pub room to the 'party room' ... the next door ... I open it ... again a room, but very, very big and wide ... a battlefield, dead, wounded, bleeding ... also sick, suicidal and others ...

What is the central element here? ... The fight ... to harm others ... to assert oneself at the expense of others ... to take what one wants ... to be unrestrained in one's will ... ... yes, this has a lot to do with my shadow, with my 'personal devil' ...

"Devil or you, Barbarossa – what can I do here to integrate this?"

"That which your Kundalini has taught you: 'look, feel, embrace'."

"Hm ... the struggle is necessary, I can see that ... wanting to win the struggle with all your might is also necessary – otherwise you might as well leave it alone ... that doesn't exclude the striving for peaceful solutions, but the striving for cooperation must not interfere with the power of self-expression and self-assertion ... o.k., that's clear so far ...

And how does it feel? ... fiery, lively, warlike ... actually simple, but I have to do it ... hm – does it take time? – Yes, but please not too much ...

And hugging? Yes, I want to become like that, I want to integrate Barbarossa ... I take him into myself ...

Let's see what that does ...

Hm, devil, is there another door? Maybe to the collective shadow, that is, to your realm?"

"Yes, there is."

"Then I want to go there too."

"O.k. ... then come!"

The devil leads me across the room to the door at the other end. It, too, leads to a hallway. The hallway is almost completely dark. The ground becomes boggy – have I already walked through a door at the end of the hallway without realizing it? It gets boggier and boggier ... pale light, slightly flat-hummocky ... reeds ... dead fire ... or fireflies? ... in any case milky-white, slightly bluish lights above the marsh ...

What is the most important thing here? ... ... skulls lie in the swamp ... skeletons ... Is death the most important thing here? ... There is something speaking to me, but I can't understand it yet – it's more like a rustling, hissing, dull whistling or something like that ... Is death speaking to me? ...

"What would be helpful here right now, devil?"

"Sit down and get quiet."

"O.K."

I sit down ... the ground is wet and swampy ... it smells faintly foul ... this is dissolution ...

"Devil – is this dissolution the shadow side of the astrological planet Neptune, which is at my ascendant?"

"Yes."

"Then this is not the collective shadow, the collective devil, but my own shadow?"

"Yes."

"If this were the collective shadow, you probably would have dissolved into this landscape by now, too, right?"

"So gradually you are beginning to understand the logic of these inner life force images ..."

"Neptune – what do you want to show me?"

"Exactly what you see."

"I don't quite understand the meaning yet."

"Feel."

"There's relaxation, letting go ... also dying ... dying in peace ... giving up one's form ... ... Is this something I'm still struggling with, Neptune?"

"Letting go in all its depth is still difficult for you, yes."

"Um – is that the all-autumn death of Osiris, who is my patron deity?"

"You feel safe with that by now – you fear the general dissolution."

"Hm ... yes, I can feel that – the 'bogging down' ... I don't want that ... And there's something wrong with that?"

"You're running from drugs, from rot, from mold, from mental illness, from dementia, from all unpleasant forms of dissolution ..."

"Um – and is that a problem in any way?"

"No – it's what you do, what you decided, what you want."

"Does that mean that the personal devil is simply made up of the things you have decided against?"

"Yes."

"Then it means that when you decide to do something, you then create an ideal, but at the same time you also create a devil – the very thing you don't want ..."

"You can look at it that way."

"Only if I didn't want anything, there would be no ideal and no shadow ... but then I wouldn't be really there and I would not be really alive ... But that means that when I express myself, I automatically also create a devil – precisely that which is the opposite of what I want ...

This means that the devil is a necessity in life: Without decisions no devil, without decisions no aliveness – and aliveness implies the devil ...

This is a completely new point of view for me ... Is then the creation of a devil in the sense of the opposite of what one has decided for, actually a problem?

How do you see it, devil?"

"It is not a problem to decide for something and thus reject other things. That doesn't prevent you at all from doing what you want – that's what enables you to want something and to achieve it.

It's only a problem if you repress something, if you don't live parts of yourself, if you develop wrong ideas, if you let yourself be guided by fear, hatred and greed."

"Um ... so there is such a thing as a 'healthy, necessary devil' and a 'harmful, disease-causing devil'?"

"You can call it that."

"I think that's enough for me for now – I need to let that sink in ... Or do you, Devil, or you, Neptune, have anything else you want to tell me?"

Neptune: "All in good time – there's no hurry."

Devil: "Yes, so it is."

"Thank you, both of you."

"You are welcome."

I walk inwardly through the two corridors, the two rooms and the pub back to the starting point and then leave the dream journey ...

"Ho!"

7. Order and Chaos

The devil represents everything that disturbs, causes chaos or runs counter to order in a kingdom or order in a monotheistic religion. One calls the devil also the "Anti-Christ", thus the antipole to Christ, who is the measure of all things in Christianity.

This Anti-Christ, Anti-King, Anti-God, this personified principle of anti-order has already some predecessors in the Neolithic Age, i.e. in the mythological-magical world view of this epoch.

A very original form is the Egyptian god-brotherpair Osiris and Seth. Osiris is the god of grain and therefore also the god of culture as well as the god of the dead due to the grain/man analogy; Seth, on the other hand, is the god of the wilderness. This is the basic opposition that arose from agriculture and animal husbandry around 8500 BC in Mesopotamia.

The graingod and god of the dead is the village in the middle, around it the gardens, then the fields and finally on the very outside the pastures – the god of the wilderness is the steppe, the desert, the forest, the mountains, the bush …

In the beginning, this was simply the world as people found it or shaped it: an island of culture in nature. In this form, this contrast has been largely preserved in Egypt, even until 600 AD: Osiris is the god of the fertile alluvial land of the Nile and Seth is the god of the desert. Seth kills Osiris in every autumn – the harvest of the grain is the death of Osiris … there it was obvious to let carry out the murder of Osiris by his antipole, thus by Seth. Therefore, however, Seth was not "evil", but just a part of the course of the things – both of human life and the grain … Even in the late time of the Egyptian empire pharaohs still named themselves after Seth and at that time "Seth-nacht" ("strength of Seth") was still a popular man's name.

It was only after the decline of the Egyptian empire that Seth began to become part of the general image of the devil.

Clearly closer to the image of the later devil than Seth was already the monster Ammut, which ate the sinners at the Egytian afterlife judgment. But even this monster was still regarded as a necessary institution – however, it was also feared.

Finally, there was a third root of the devil in Egypt: the goddess Isfet, who embodied non-rightness.

In the Egyptian religion, however, there has never been a "real devil".

An interesting development can be seen in Osiris. He is the god of the dead and the god of grain. All Egyptians wished to become like Osiris in the afterlife judgment, to become an Osiris, to become Osiris. Osiris was the ideal and the hope and the embodiment of rightness.

Around 1500 AD in Europe, a completely different image had emerged from the parable between the death of men and the harvest of grain: the scythe-man. As a skeleton he is death, as a man with a scythe he is the harvester who "kills" the grain.

While Osiris has been the image of hope, the reaper has been the image of terror … Hope and fear of death have been represented with the same image, which shows how much the fear of death can shape a parable and transform it into its opposite.

Through this fear, the image of the longed-for god Osiris has become the dreaded image of the reaper …

Again, another version of the opposition of order and chaos is found in the two Greek gods Apollo and Dionysus. Apollo is the order, meditation, rhythm, the sun, the light, the radiant – Dionysos is the creative chaos, ecstasy, the breaking of all rules, the gloomy, incomprehensible …

Here the contrast is different from Osiris and Seth: they are the two basic methods of the shaman's journey to the otherworld (meditation and ecstasy) and thus also of the change of consciousness.

In meditation, one becomes more and more silent – it is the imitation of death, in which the soul discards its body and psyche and becomes itself again without a shell.

In ecstasy one becomes louder and louder – it is the dance, the hunt, the completely one-directed activity, by which the soul finally radiates unhindered through the psyche to the outside and appears completely as itself in the world.

Apollo and Dionysos have the same goal, but strive for it with exactly opposite methods: Apollo with the production of the perfect order – Dionysos with the dissolution of any order.

Now Dionysos is by no means the devil, but he comes quite close to him by his character …

Again another concept is found in the Kabbalistic Tree of Life in Jewish mysticism, which has been formulated in its essential features about 800 AD, but whose roots reach far back into the pre-Christian mythology.

There are two Trees of Life: one of them consists of the 11 Sephiroth, which represent the right, wholesome order and thus correspond to the Egyptian goddess Ma'at – the other of these two Trees of Life consists of the 11 Qliphoth, which represent the not-right, sick disorder and thus correspond to the Egyptian goddess Isfet. This second Tree of Life is more a "Tree of Death". Probably these two trees appear in the Bible as the "Tree of Life" and the "Tree of Knowledge of Good and Evil".

The contemporary interpretation of these two systems (Sephiroth and Qliphoth) depends, of course, very much on the worldview of the person concerned: it ranges from "order and disorder" to "God and Devil as opponents" to "God and Devil as equal poles."

No matter which of these interpretations one may prefer, however, the Qliphoth always remain an "anatomy of the devil", so to speak.

Again another version of the opposition "order and chaos" is the Hindhuistic "Samadhi and Karma" or the Buddhistic "Nirvana and Samsara".

The Samadhi and the Nirvana are the redeemed, suffering-free state, which is described differently by Hindhuists and Buddhists, but is nevertheless for both the right, desirable state.

Karma is the causes of the suffering one experiences, samsara is living in suffering – both are ultimately seen as the "evil" to be avoided. It is interesting to note that in both cases, the suffering is seen as self-inflicted and the person is seen as autonomous and thus able to end that suffering as well. Ultimately, this difference consists in the fact that in the monotheistic religions, i.e. above all in Judaism, Christianity and Islam, the "legal basis" for the origin of suffering is seen in the will and the law of the One God, whereas Hindhuism and Buddhism see the cause of suffering rather in a form of "spiritual laws of nature".

Therefore, in India also the manifold and luxuriantly painted pictures of suffering in this world and in the hereafter, as well as the gods causing this suffering in the hereafter, have in the end not so much the character of independent beings, but more the character of embodiments of natural laws.

This leads to the fact that in Hindhuism and Buddhism man does not have to fight against a devil, but only has to take care of world-knowledge and self-knowledge and thereby to develop further and to become free of suffering.

There are also in Hindhuism feared deities like the destruction goddess Kali or the death god Yama, but they are never "evil" in themselves and therefore a form of the devil – they always result from the "spiritual laws of nature" and their observance or non-observance by the individual human being.

Buddhism in particular emphasizes that all the monsters in their religion, called "raging and blood-drinking deities", are all ultimately properties of an enlightened person, such as the willingness to see the world as it is – boundless equanimity, that is, boundless serenity. As long as one has not yet fully acquired this ability, one will gradually see more and more, but one will be horrified at what one sees – especially at what one sees in oneself. However, when one has attained perfect affirmation, one can look at everything with a smile – even on oneself.

"God and Devil" as "order and chaos" can be evaluated and understood quite differently depending on one's worldview: from the stone on the path that one stubs one's toe on, to the enemy one has to fight, to a fundamental duality in the world consisting of the personally wanted and the personally unwanted.

The fear of the devil is greatest in those religions in which the devil is the enemy of the One God and disturbs his intentions and tempts people to consequencial actions. These religions in which the devil plays the greatest role are Judaism, Christianity and Islam.

The devil thrives only in monotheism …

7th Dream Journey to the Devil

"Hello devil – did I get that right about you and monotheism?"

"We already had that ... without an absolute ruler in heaven and his deputy on earth, no hardness arises ... and thus no devil, who must be destroyed at all costs."

"Um ... kingship and monotheism, which is the religious reflection of kingship, correspond in man to the phallic phase, in which man creates the 'I!!!' of the phallic phase from the 'yes' of the oral phase and from the 'no!' of the anal phase. Can I conclude from this that for the creation of the I it is necessary to create also a devil? So a figure which represents everything what one does not want, what one has not decided for? Can one, without creating a devil, not become independent at all?"

"You see this correctly in principle, but you evaluate it wrongly."

"Er ...?"

"The distinction of 'wanted' and 'rejected' is necessary as an orientation – this distinction and especially this decision are the basis for you to develop an ego. You need the 'good' and the 'bad' – otherwise you don't know who you are and what you want. It is also necessary to fight to achieve what you want and to prevent what you don't want.

But that doesn't mean that you have to declare what you don't want to be the 'general evil' that you have to destroy everywhere. Nor does it mean that you must become the supreme ruler of the entire galaxy in order to achieve what you want to achieve."

"So the will needs a distinction in 'light' and 'dark'?"

"This distinction is the basis of the will – the 'Yes' of the baby and the 'No!' of the toddler only make it possible to develop a will, i.e. an 'I!!!'."

"Um ... the 'Yes' of the baby corresponds to the security in the sweat lodge with the mother goddess in the Old Stone Age and the 'No!' of the toddler corresponds to the view of the wilderness in the New Stone Age ... whereby finally the 'I!!!' of the 'inner king' can emerge ..."

"Yes."

"So the devil is necessary for one's ego to gain stability, strength and radiance ... without the devil, no persuasive power in life ... Look at that! Who would have thought it?! ... ... I find it amazing, where all these contemplations lead to – especially these dream journeys ...

Am I missing something important?"

"You could look at how the story of a single person continues and what role I play in it."

"Um, yes ... I could have thought of that myself – after all, that is normally my usual procedure ...

So: There are first of all the 'Yes' of the oral phase (that corresponds to the Paleolithic) and then the 'No!' of the anal phase (that corresponds to the Neolithic), from whose connection then the 'I!!!' of the phallic phase arises (that corresponds to kingship).

O.k. – and then: the genital phase ... In puberty one has ideally the 'I!!!' as a solid foundation and looks from there on the world – this corresponds to materialism with its emphasis on science and technology. This is a 'You?'

The answer to this 'You?' can be given in a safe and sustainable way, if one has clearly recognized beforehand what one wants, thus the 'Yes', and if one has clearly recognized what one does not want, thus the 'No!'. In the Paleolithic Age, one lives in nature as part of nature and agrees with nature as it is all that is there ... In the Neolithic Age, one creates the islands of culture in nature and defends them against nature.

One will look for a 'You?' in the genital phase, which has the same goals and ideals and consequently the same dislikes and therefore the same devil. The clearer both know what they want and the clearer they show that to the other, the greater the chance that they will find someone to match with.

O.k. ... the adult phase. ... Now the adolescent has grown up and started a family – the 'I!!!' and the 'You?" has now become a 'We'. This is collectively the phase of globalization, which started approximately with the founding of the UN around 1942. It is based on the insight into the necessity of the general cooperation on our earth.

What role does the devil play in this? It is easy to see: It became clear that we could exterminate ourselves as humanity through wars, nuclear wars, overpopulation, environmental pollution, global warming, species extinction, resource consumption, unrestrained economic growth, and so on. So the devil in this case was the image of our collective death. The realization of this very real possibility is what we said 'No!' to ... so this is the devil we want to avoid concretizing and realizing.

Hm – the devil seems to be an almost necessary component of our development ... I would not have expected that ...

The ideal of this individual phase or this collective epoch would be the dissolution of the borders: to carry the whole in responsibility and to be carried by the whole in trust.

The next stage of individual and collective development: the tutorial phase. ... In it, the children are out of the house and one undertakes journeys, learns new things, teaches others one's own knowledge, writes books, etc. This is an 'Other ...'

Collectively, this phase is still in the future – in it probably many new variants of the first stable form of coexistence of people on Earth will emerge, which are developed in the adult phase, that is, during globalization.

What is the devil there? The being fixed to a single role? Then the ideal would be to get to know the diversity of the world ...

And the last developmental step: the gerontic phase ... The old man looks at the world, experiences himself as part of the whole – and mankind as a collective will probably also experience itself as a unity. Then the 'We.' and the 'Other ...' has become an all-encompassing 'All'.

What is the devil here? The rejection of a part of the world? Probably ... Does this dissolve the devil in the end, because one agrees to the whole? At least that sounds like it ... shortly after that one dissolves oneself with one's own death – so it fits that before that one also expands one's own will and reduces one's preferences and takes the world as it is ... well, that's ultimately also what Buddha did ...

In the oral phase (0-1 year) and in the Paleolithic period
      the ideal is the abundance
      and the devil the lack,
            which gives rise to the urge of the addict
            and the retreat of the ascetic.

In the anal phase (1-3 years) and in the Neolithic period
      the ideal is the strength and the clarity
      and the devil the power,
            the power of the perpetrator
            and the powerlessness of the victim.

In the phallic phase (3-12 years) and in kingship
      the ideal is self-love
      and the devil is self-doubt
            which causes the megalomania of the star
            and the inferiority complex of the fan.

These first three phases create the three basic qualities of abundance, strength and self-love – or lack, power and self-doubt. The following four phases vary these qualities in new contexts.

In the genital phase (about 12-21 years) and in materialism
      the ideal is self-expression
      and the devil is self-uncertainty,
            which is the urge of the inconsiderate
            and the despondency of the fearful.

In the adult phase (about 21-58 years) and in globalism
      the ideal is cooperation
      and the devil the threatening failure of the community,
            the dominance of the one refusing closeness
            and the subordination of the one asking for closeness.

In the tutorial phase (about 58-70 years) and in the future I
      the ideal is the guiding
      and the devil the compulsion,
            the roar of the commanding
            and the silence of the seeker of support.

In the gerontic phase (about from 70 years onward) and in the future II
      the ideal is the unifying
      and the devil the division,
            which is the destruction by the egoist
            and the clinging of the altruist.

What do you think, devil, of what I've been thinking about now?"
"That's enough for now – we'll have a few more conversations ..."
"Thank you! Thank you so much!"
"You're welcome ... it's not that often that someone thanks me ..."
"I do from the bottom of my heart! ... ... Ho!"

8. The God of the Wilderness

Well – actually this topic has already been talked about, but there are some more aspects to discover here.

The god of the wilderness is the antithesis to the god of the grain, to the god of the cattle, to the god of the villages … he is the wild, disordered – he is what man has not yet subdued on the earth … Well, this aspect of the devil doesn't have too much power nowadays, after all …

In the kingdom-epoch the god of the wilderness became also the god of the foreign lands, thus the god of the foreigners – and thus tends to be the god of the enemies.

This development can be observed e.g. with the Egyptian god Seth. Also the North-Germans and especially the Vikings equated the non-Vikings, i.e. all peoples they plundered, with the giants killed by the thundergod Thor. In this context, xenophobia is still seen as something natural – here the "I" was still vehemently opposed to the "non-I" and thus one's own people against the other peoples, the "we" against the "non-we".

For the era of globalization, this is an extremely obstructive attitude if we want to secure our survival on this planet.

Alongside this "us and them" thinking, however, early cultures also had the commandment of hospitality that applied to all people …

Another aspect of the wilderness god is simply his wildness – he lives his feelings and instincts uninhibitedly, is eager, does not look ahead, is destructive, does not fit in …

This wildness is on the one hand a great emotional liveliness, but on the other hand also a knee-jerk orientation in the world – he lacks the moment of pause between stimulus and reaction, which constitutes the conscious ego.

All these wilderness and chaos gods ultimately fail … the Egyptian Seth, the Germanic Loki, the coyote of the Plains Indians, the spider god Iktomi of the Dakota Indians, the West African spider man Anansi, and so on. They lack the calm overall view and trick themselves …

The wilderness aspect of the devil is often also associated with his drives, instincts and with his exaggerated sexuality. On the one hand he is cunning, but on the other hand he is so much controlled by his instincts and drives that he overlooks something important which causes his plans to fail.

This aspect of the devil is actually an image of deterrence, that is, a depiction of mistakes that one might commit and that one would rather avoid.

One can also consider ecstasy as an aspect of wildness – after all, one reaches this state of single-mindedness by wild dances, among other things. However, these dances, these chants and mantras also all have a very ordered aspect, as they are all completely directed towards a single goal – e.g. the invocation of a deity.

Therefore, ecstasy belongs to wildness only at first glance because of its great power. But this great power is directed – it can also be the intimate prayer of a priest before a statue of his god.

Another possible aspect of wildness is intoxication, which is caused by drugs. In it, conscious control is relinquished and one abandons oneself to a momentum brought about by the drug in one's own body and consciousness.

Since both the epoch of kingdom and the epoch of materialism are characterized by a high degree of order, control, and predictability, most drugs are considered disruptive and harmful and are therefore banned. They are officially "evil" and thus "devil's work."

8th Dream Journey to the Devil

"Did I miss anything else in the wildness, devil?"
"You are missing it a little ..."
"Er, yes ... wildness makes demanding, dominant and influential – that is the extreme of the addict, the perpetrator and the star ... I am rather on the side of the ascetic, the victim and the fan, even if I increasingly work my way out of it ...
But I meant more if you can say or show me something more general about this."
"The general is useless if you don't see your own."
"Yes, well ... one could argue that an example is usually the most illustrative. Where am I being wild?"
"When you improvise music, when you dance, when you roam through the forest ..."
"These are all things that I usually do alone ..."
"That's your problem – you haven't integrated your wildness, you live it solo, so almost secretly, you don't think your wildness is socially acceptable, you think everyone will leave you if you get wild ... You're even embarrassed sometimes by the loud screams of your girlfriends when she orgasms ..."
"O.k. ... now you're getting pretty private ..."
"You can change only if you go to the essence ..."

53

"Yes, well ... So wildness is unbridled self-expression ... without regard for others ... at least without fear of the reactions of others ... Um – can it be that wildness is need-oriented and not person-oriented?"

"The devil is always need-oriented ..."

"At least, if he has a Scorpio Ascendant ..."

"Person-orientation is the attitude of the ascetic, the victim, and the fan – need-orientation is the attitude of the addict, the abuser, and the star."

"Oh – I hadn't noticed that ... yes, that's right ... And you are need-oriented because you are more of the addict/perpetrator/star type?"

"In most cases, I am of that type, yes. ... Otherwise I would be powerless ..."

"Then what is the wholesome attitude in the middle between these two extremes? ... Probably the ability to fulfill one's own needs and at the same time to perceive other people and to take their needs into account ... in other words, cooperation ... trust and responsibility – but in autonomy ...

Is there anything more to say about this?"

"Don't forget that insights are only useful if you put them into action."

"Yes ... o.k. ... I guess that's true ... ... Thank you, devil."

"You're welcome."

"Ho!"

9. The God of the Witches

The devil is often considered the god of witches and pagans in general. The devil is conceived from the point of view of the "right religion" as the god of the "wrong religion" … This is ultimately the same principle as in kingship: one's own "right" people and the other, "wrong" peoples by whom one is threatened …

The witches were originally the seers and priestesses especially of the Germans and to a lesser extent of the Celts and Slavs. They were reinterpreted as witches by the Christian missionaries – but they could build on the already existing fear of the Germanic underworld goddess Hel and of the Slavic underworld goddess Babajaga … the missionaries did not have to start from scratch with the "demonization".

For a Christian missionary, the priests and priestesses of the religion in the place where they wanted to convert people to Christianity were, of course, the main enemies – their direct counterpart who represented a different worldview. Therefore, if possible, this priesthood had to be killed first – already in the Old Testament Elijah, with God's help, defeated the priests of Ba'al in a magic contest and then had them all killed.

The magic contest used to be the usual method to find out which god was the more powerful and therefore the "right god". This procedure was a variant of the widespread ordeal by duel.

However, some victors dealt with the defeated in a more "Christian" way and did not kill them – such as the Tibetan Buddhist Yogi Milarepa after defeating a Bön shaman or a hypocritical Buddhist priest in a magic contest.

Character assassination as a preparation for real assassination is a commonly popular method: if you portray your enemies as monsters, it is easier to fight against them and kill them …

So the missionaries portrayed the Germanic priestesses as evil women (damage spells), as causers of all diseases ("Hexenschuß" = lumbago), as child-eaters ("Hansel and Gretel"), as poisoners ("Snow White"), as unfaithful wives ("ride to the Blocksberg" and "to be intimate with the devil") etc..

Within the framework of this smear campaign, everything was then also reinterpreted in a suitable way: a broom became a disguised seeress staff, the fertility god Freyr with his large penis became the devil, the fertility festivals became Walpurgis Night, the hill grave where the seeresses asked the ancestors for advice and help became the Blocksberg, the ritual fires became the fire in the oven in which the witches roasted children, and so on.

One could also call this "religious-political propaganda". Thereby one transferred all qualities, abilities and activities, which one rejected (thus the devil of the own world view), on the priesthood of the peoples, which had another faith than oneself.

55

However, one must distinguish between the different religions – not all of them proceeded in the same way:

Judaism never proselytized on a large scale – even though there are some brutal scenes in the Old Testament when dealing with people of other faiths.

Christianity proselytized intensely and demonized everything non-Christian. They were the most extreme in this respect.

Islam regarded Judaism and Christianity as monotheistic religions of revelation ("book religions") and thus as precursors of Islam and therefore granted them a certain freedom.

Hindhuism, with its multitude of deities and cults, is largely tolerant and accepts the diversity of opinions and ways.

Buddhism has remained almost always peace-loving – only the "demons" in areas where Buddhists have preached have been subdued and committed to the protection of Buddhism.

The other religions, all of which were not as distinctly monotheistic or focused on a single principle as Buddhism, do not have the claim of missionization and world domination – on the contrary, they are often the religion of a clan or a people, still strongly influenced by the connection to the ancestors and to the gods of a landscape. They are to some extend the "private religion" of a tribe.

The devil as the "god of the non-Christians" is, as this definition suggests, primarily a Christian phenomenon.

As usual, the rituals of the witches on the Blocksberg were depicted as repulsive as in any way possible – with child sacrifices, kisses of the witches on the anus of the devil and more of the like …

9th Dream Journey to the Devil

"Hello devil – could we say that you are a Christian figure?"
"Under the name 'devil' I am certainly a Christian figure and I also play the greatest role in Christianity. But I am known, for example, in Judaism and in Christianity as 'Satan' and in Islam as 'Shaitan' … I am more universal than each of the three

great monotheistic religions and their 'One God' ...

The name 'Satan' is Hebrew and means 'adversary'. So I am the main figure in the monotheistic world religions – all believe in me, but always only a part in Yahweh, God or Allah ... whereby most of them don't see that Yahweh, God and Allah are only three names for the same being – and for the same principle ... namely for the ideal, the 'almighty and all-knowing and just king in heaven'. And I am that which does not suit them ..."

"Um ... it's interesting that you appear in the three monotheistic religions under the same name ...

There are some other names like e.g. 'Ahriman' in the Zend Avesta in Persia, where you are the opponent of the supreme god Ahura Mazda – at least in the form, how Zarathustra has represented this. Before, this opponent was called 'Angra Mainyu', i.e. 'evil spirit', which is ultimately identical in meaning with 'Satan', i.e. 'opponent'. So you are simply what is not wanted by the prevailing opinion.

This is so plain and obvious that I know nothing more to ask about it now ... do you want to say anything more about it, devil?"

"No."

"Thank you."

"You're welcome."

"Ho!"

10. Christ's Rivals

The pagan priests have been a problem for the Christian priests – the "heathen competitors." They have been reinterpreted as witches and evil sorcerers – the "servants of the devil."

Likewise, the pagan gods have been a problem – the "pagan competitors". They were summarized to the devil himself.

Then there were the "leaders of the mysteries". Most of them were not particularly dangerous to Christianity. The "mysteries of the Christians" were the Lord's Supper – a very simple variant of the mysteries of Eleusis, of Samothrake, of Sol invictus, of the teachings of Buddha, of Lao-tse, etc.

However, there were two mystery leaders who posed a problem for missionary work in Central and Northern Europe: Odin and Cernunnos. Both were originally shamans who guided the afterlife journey. When the mysteries and wisdom teachings emerged around 600 B.C. from China to Rome, the Celts and the Germanic tribes gave the task of guiding their own mysteries, which they modeled after the mysteries in the Mediterranean, to Cernunnos and Odin, respectively.

Since these two shamans thereby received the function of an archetype, they ascended to gods – i.e. they received a position exactly corresponding to that of Christ in Christianity. The man who shows the way became the god to whom one wanted to become like.

The same thing happened 2500 years before with Osiris: The archetype of the dead man reborn in the afterlife became the reborn god with whom everyone identified.

Thus, Cernunnos and Odin were particularly dangerous figures in terms of Christian missionary work – they were too similar to Christ. Like Christ, both were other-worldly travelers, mystery leaders, gods of the dead, and heralds (Odin) or archetypes (Odin and Cernunnos) of a religion.

Therefore, both were equated with the devil:

> Cernunnos as a god with deer antlers and a snake in his hand could be equated quite easily with the horned devil and the snake-shaped devil.
>
> However, there are also representations in which Christ converses with Cernunnos – but this is very rare. In the Eadwine Psalter, written around 1160 AD in Canterbury in southeast England, Christ talks to a Cernunnos shaman (demon?) with bird feet about the (psychotropic?) plants or mushrooms in his hands.
>
> Odin was re-styled as the god of war and the god of the dead to be the leader of the army of the dead or the "Wild Hunt" so that everyone began to fear him.

It is interesting that Odin was reinterpreted here from the god of war to the god of the hunt – did they want to avoid that Odin got too much power by the image of a regular army?

The Celtic stag god and also the Germanic sunstag were, because they were very popular, reinterpreted to "St. Hubert with the stag" – where this stag carries the sun (like the Germanic stag) and the cross of Christ in his antlers.

A similar procedure as with the stag god was applied to the mother-goddess, who, being such a deeply rooted image, could not be reinterpreted as a demon: the mother-goddesses in the various religions missionized by the Christians were simply replaced by Mary. The most important reinterpretation was from Isis to Mary, since Isis had been the most important goddess in the Mediterranean in the centuries before and after the birth of Christ.

10th Dream Journey to the Devil

"What is your relationship with Christ, Cernunnos and Odin, Devil?"

"A creative question, even if you asked it from a somewhat chaotic inner state ... You first talked and then thought. You actually wanted to ask about the relationship between Christ, Cernunnos and Odin, didn't you?"

"Um ... yes ... after everything what I have experienced so far in the area of the gods, there are no enmities there ... I have seen once in a vision Christ and Krishna like brothers next to each other ... and on a dream journey I have visited a meeting of all the Indo-Germanic forge gods ... and I had still some more similar experiences ... and besides Christ, Cernunnos and Odin have in their respective religions very similar tasks.

But now I seem to have asked a creative question by my hasty speech ..."

"I have nothing against Christ, Cernunnos and Odin – they are just as real as I am ... and I am just as real as they are. We exist."

"Um ... is the principle of 'enmity' too humanly conceived?"

"I am not a being who needs to defend his own existence, or who would need omni-potence for his well-being."

"Are Christ, Cernunnos and Odin, as well as Buddha, Lao-tse, Jaina, Zarathustra, Pythagoras, Patanjali, Zalmoxis, etc., all ultimately beings who simply show a way to go?"

"That sounds pretty good."

"And you embody the deviation from that path?"

"Yes."

"Actually, there's nothing wrong with that ... seeing where the path is that you want to go, and at the same time seeing the swamp to the left and the abyss to the right of that path, is, after all, decidedly helpful and useful. ... Does the problem begin when we believe that it is not we who decide which way to go, but when we believe that You have made us go a certain way?"

"Yes – this is the basic error concerning my being: you have your free decision and I only show you the consequences of your decisions. If you believe that you are 'good' and that I want to seduce you to 'evil', you have given up your autonomy ... then you no longer see that it is you who decides and goes – then you have given up being true to yourself and then you have sold your freedom to me ..."

"Now that's a completely different version of 'selling your own soul to the devil' than usual ... it sounds much more logical this way ....

That actually means that you are working with Christ, doesn't it? Christ and the other wisdom teachers show a way and you show the possible potholes on this way ..."

"Yes ... and who is doing 'evil'? Am I standing in the dark alley and robbing an old man of his money or am I the one raping a woman there? No – it is you yourselves! And if you believe that I made you do it, then you have given up your freedom. You carry repressed desires inside of you and you go the most different ways and think the most different things are right... but that is inside of you and that is what you do – that has nothing to do with me. It is complete nonsense that the devil has brought evil into the world! I am nothing else than the image of what you do not want – and I have not created what you do not want ... that has all been there already – especially in yourselves as your own cruelty or your greed and your errors, your hatred, your megalomania, your addiction and what else there is ...

I am your scapegoat, whom you put the blame on! This is really comfortable ... and it makes you dependent, you believe yourselves to be dependent on me, you give me your freedom and live as if you would be my slaves ... But you have created me yourselves: as the image of what you don't want ... And you have not taken the time to really look exactly what you actually want, who you really are. 'Do what you want' – that's it, that's what frees you ... and that's laborious, because for that you have to explore yourself first, you need courage to do things differently than the others, for that you have to develop independence and sincerity and vulnerability and many other things ... How easy it is to say that the devil is to blame for everything ... With this kind of comfort you will never be happy and be able to express radiantly what you really are!"

... ...

"Now that was one of the most convincing sermons I have ever heard – and the devil was the speaker in the pulpit ...

You always make new things clear to me, dear devil – if I may call you so ..."

"Love your shadow – then you will become complete, true and free."

"Whew ... yes ... you're probably right ... ... Thank you, devil, for all that you're telling me!"

"If you like – more about it soon."

"Yes, gladly ... ... Ho!"

11.   The Accuser

If you look at the ancient texts about the devil in Judaism, Christianity and Islam, you will find another aspect of the devil: the accuser at the afterlife court.

This court had become necessary because in this world things are obviously not very just – consequently God had to be either unjust or not almighty … this dilemma could only be solved by claiming that the life in this world was followed by a final trial in the hereafter.

The two unpleasant figures for the accused at such a trial are the prosecutor and the executioner.

The executioner first appears as the monster Ammut in the afterlife hall of Osiris, where the heart of the dead is weighed against the feather of the goddess of rightness Ma'at. He later became the devil who tortures in the underworld the dead who had not lived righteously in the Christian way.

The role of the accuser did not yet exist in ancient Egypt. The righteousness of the dead, i.e. his observance of the Ma'at in his life was only checked by the jackal god Anubis with the help of the feather/heart scales and the result was then written down by the ibis god Thot. Although Osiris officially presided over this and Ma'at herself was also present, both are almost completely passive in this heart examination.

However, since the afterlife court was increasingly aligned with the earthly courts, the accuser is also found among the Jews early on: Satan. He is an angel whose name means "adversary, enemy", also in the legal sense of "accuser". In this function he appears, for example, in the Old Testament in the Book of Job. Even in the 14th century AC, the motif of the angel Satan as the accuser of people at the judgment in the otherworld, i.e. in the Last Judgment, was still very popular in Christianity. In this context, Satan is not evil himself, but only performs a function that is distinctly unpleasant for people.

Already in the Book of Job, Satan's activity as an accuser expanded to that of an active seducer: he not only accuses those who have already sinned, but he tests their moral steadfastness by either seducing them or by tormenting them. Here Satan has become a kind of "agent provocateur", an undercover agent, a saboteur – which, by the way, are all Scorpio professions …

Satan also tests Jesus' steadfastness by offering him that if he, Christ, kneels before him, Satan, he will give him all the kingdoms of the world.

In Islam, too, Satan, who is called "Shaitan" there, has this dual function of accuser and deceiver.

In both Judaism and Islam, God is the only reality and the devil is, so to speak, God's employee with special responsibilities. In Christianity and in many Persian religions, on the other hand, God and the devil often stand side by side like two poles more or less equal and equally strong, waging an endless battle against each other. This dualism is another way to explain the injustice in the world – renouncing the dogma of God's omnipotence.

This dualism corresponds to the view of the Scorpion … and in this dual world view the devil also has by far the greatest power … Here he is not only the unwanted, the accuser, the seducer and the executioner, but the principle cf destruction.

In the Jewish tradition Satan wears wings as an angel and consequently can also fly, but he can also appear as a bird (soul bird), stag or he-goat (herd animal → procreation) as well as a woman or a man.

Here we find once again the development, so frequent in mythology, from an element in an unpleasant context to a cause of this unpleasantness: the accuser becomes the devil, thus the cause of the punishment – and thus the evil …

An understandable, but already strange distortion of the facts – just the principle of the scapegoat, which one needs with most repressions of the self-blame of one's own situation, in order to be able to repress this self-blame effectively … … … with which one also gives up one's own sincerity, independence and freedom – because one no longer sees that one is the cause for one's own life.

<u>11th Dream Journey to the Devil</u>

"Would you like to say something about your accuser role, devil?"

"I wake you up. I kick you in the shins when you do something that doesn't lead where you want to go. I'm not the accuser in the service of a domineering God – I'm the one who shows you that you're on the wrong path, that you're not going to reach your destination that way."

"I know this Principle from 'Conversations with God.' In that book, God says that he does not interfere with free will, but that He can say that if you go north from the U.S., you will not get to Mexico as fast. Also, God evaluates 'wrong' or 'right' only in terms of the path you take to get to your destination. Are you therefore 'God's corrective instructions', so to speak?"

"That's rather misleadingly worded, Harry – 'corrective instructions' sounds as if there's someone in charge, as if there's someone who's the ruler ... but I'm just showing you what won't work. It's nonsense to sleep when you're hungry ... and it's nonsense to drink when you actually want to have sex."

"Yes, you put it more clearly. ... Then your 'accuser role' is already a twisting of your character within a worldview shaped by kingdom?"

"That was only the effort to present the hereafter as a parallel world to this world – with the same laws, institutions and procedures as in this world. But the accuser, after all, is not too far removed from pointing out procedures that don't work."

"And the 'seducer role'?"

"It's nonsense. I have no concern of my own for you – I don't want you to do this and not do that. You decide how you want to live – both individually and collectively. I have nothing to do with that. If you don't want murder, then don't murder – it's that simple. If you think murder is perfectly okay, then do it – I have no preferences there."

"You're giving us back our responsibility over our own lives ..."

"Yes. I'm just the image inside you of what you don't want – officially ... because secretly many of you want a lot of things that you don't outwardly admit to. Therefore, I am also the image of what you want, but what you do not admit either to yourselves or to others. That is the most dangerous part: the repressed part of your will, the immoral shadowy figures in your psyche, which then break out from time to time and in most cases cause suffering to yourself and others, because in these outbursts you are no longer the sovereign captain of your own ship, but are only tossed to and fro by the waves of your repressed and now broken-out feelings."

"Actually you are a helper in our own healing ... when we look at you and talk to you, we can see what we have repressed in ourselves – so you showed me Barbarossa, my repressed Mars.

... ...

Thank you, devil ... this feels as if we would increasingly become friends – as far as one can say that of a being like you ..."

"From a being like me?"

"Well, you are actually a god ... and can a human and a god be friends?"

"It's different from a friendship between two humans, but why shouldn't it be possible? It enriches both of us and we both enjoy our meeting and we enjoy meeting each other ... Then why shouldn't it be called a friendship?"

"Um ... You surprise me again ... a god doesn't have a psyche after all ... then how can he have preferences and rejoice and enjoy something?"

"A god, of course, doesn't have a human psyche – and consequently neither do I, but a god has a character and consequently things that suit him and things that don't suit him ... The 'tone' of a deity and the 'tone' of a human being, when sounded together, form a certain interval that has a certain sound, a certain color ... why shouldn't they both be able to experience and enjoy that?"

"You are constantly making me aware of new things that I have not questioned, considered or recognized so far ... What you are saying fits with what I have experienced with deities so far – they do have 'personal reactions', if I may put it that way ... I have not yet perceived joy or friendship with them, but definitely sympathy, striking reactions, self-fidelity and some other things ... Yes, I think you are right with what *you have said there ... Then let us be friends!"*

"Gladly! It will do you good!"

"And you?"

"I enjoy this conversation with you."

"Why is that?"

"I experience myself in them."

"Oh..."

"Does that surprise you?"

"When I think about it like that, it's perfectly logical, but it's something I've never thought about before....

Thank you, friend devil!"

"You're welcome, friend Harry!"

"My goodness – I had no idea where writing this book would take me! ... ... But it's good – very good, in fact! ... ... Ho!"

12. The Name of the Devil

The oldest name of the devil is "Satan," meaning "adversary, enemy, accuser."

"Samael" seems to be a variant or the precursor of the name "Satan".

"Iblis" is primarily a devil's name in Islam. This devil also seems to be identical with Satan.

The name "devil" is probably derived from the Latin "diabolus", which comes from the Greek "diabolos" and means "slanderer, adversary" and thus is probably simply a Greek translation of the name "Satan" ("adversary, accuser"). If one changes the three stem consonants in the usual way in Germanic language development, i.e. "d→t", "b→f" and "l remains l", then "diabolus" becomes "tiafolus", which with abbreviated vowels then becomes "teufelus" and with omission of the ending becomes the German word "Teufel". From "diabolus" to "devil" it's also not a long way – the "b" is often changed into a "v".
 It would be conceivable that there is also a relationship with the German word "übel" or the English "evil" of the same meaning. The origin of these two words is not clarified. The devil (German: "Teufel") could also be "Der Üble" and "the evil" – then the adjective "übel" or "evil" would have been derived from the wrong interpretation of the name "devil" as "to evil", thus as "Der Üble".

The name "Lucifer" means "light-bringer" – this is Venus as the "morning star". Possibly this name originated from the misunderstanding of a Bible passage in which the king of Babylon was compared to the morning star that sets when the sun comes – which could be interpreted as "the devil goes when Christ comes".

"Phosphoros" means "light bearer" and is probably a variant of the name "Lucifer".

"Belial" is probably a variant of the Mesopotamian "Ba'al" for "Lord, God, King, Sun", with which, among other things, the name "Beli" of the Germanic sun giant and the name "Bel" or "Belenus" of the Celtic sungod are also related. "Belial" is therefore quite probably the reinterpretation of an ancient sungod name into a devil name.

"Beelzebub" is usually translated (as a mockery of the name of a pagan god) as "Lord of the Flies" or "Lord of Feces," but it actually means "Exalted Lord" ("Ba'al Zebu"). He was originally a city god of the Philistines. He was considered the second highest devil after Satan in the Middle Ages.

"Asasel", who is also called Azazil, is said to have taught people how to make weapons, similar to the Greek Prometheus. His name denoted the wasteland where the Jews sacrificed a goat to which the sins of all Jews were transferred – that is, the "sacrificial place of the scapegoat."

"Asmodaeus" is a devil, of forbidden sexuality. He is a variant of Aeshma, the Persian demon of anger, greed and lust.

"Baphomet" has been worshipped by the Templars and some others. He is usually depicted as a cross-legged man with a goat's head and female breasts. There are many explanations of his name, but none of them is reasonably certain to be the correct one – the interpretation of his nature is correspondingly uncertain. In any case he seems to have something to do with initiations.

These names all agree with the previous observations on the nature of the devil.

12th Dream Journey to the Devil

"Would you like to say something about these names, devil?"
"No ... boring ..."
"Er ... yes, well ... thank you ... ... Ho!"

13. God Father and the Fathers

The Christian priests had a big problem during the missionary work in Northern and Central Europe: people trusted the help and advice of their ancestors in the burial mounds.

Now, how to explain to the people of that time that their own dead fathers were wrong and evil and that they had to turn to the one God Father in Heaven and not to their real fathers for advice and help? This problem was really not easy to solve …

But ways and means were found to achieve the demonization of the ancestral spirits:

> A central point was, of course, the fear of death, which could be transferred to the spirits of the dead. The missionaries succeeded well – even today many people do not like to go to a cemetery at night …

> Further also already from the Germanic people the invocations of the spirits of the dead in the late time of the Germanic religion were sometimes, even if only rarely, represented as something creepy - whereby it cannot be said whether this creepy feeling was not already taken over from Christianity.

> The ancestors in herdanimal/human-mixed form were reinterpreted as animal demons, from which then the devil arose.

> Then there were already horror images of the afterlife goddess Hel, which one could reinterpret to "the devil's grandmother".

> From the Hel-dog, which guarded the dead, one could easily make a hellish dog, which threatened the dead – already the Greek Cerberus had become a fear figure.

> The evocation of the dead from their burial mounds, i.e. necromancy, was gradually given more and more gruesome associations, so that finally in the Occident necromancy became the most frightening thing one could do – although the fear of the spirit of a dead person who had been well-disposed to oneself during his life is actually completely absurd.

> In the Neolithic Age in Mesopotamia, people even placed the skulls of the dead in niches in the wall of the dwelling house, so that they could contact the spirits of the dead in question at any time via these skulls.

> To the Germanic sungod and father of the gods Tyr, feet and hands of clay were offered as gifts at crossroads, because Tyr's hands, feet and head were cut off at his death in the evening – the sacrifice was supposed to cause Tyr,

i.e. the sun, to return in the morning. Possibly crossroads were chosen for this sacrifice, because the circle with an equal-armed cross in it was the symbol of the sun.

The medieval custom of summoning the dead as well as demons and the devil at nightly crossroads probably originated from this tradition.

Fortunately, however, the trust in the spirits of the dead could not be completely eradicated, as shown, among others, by spiritualism and today's family constellations.

13ᵗʰ Dream Journey to the Devil

"Hello devil ... um, tell me – do you perhaps have another more suitable name than 'devil'? After all, the idea that you are 'evil' is very distinct."

"Stick with 'devil', everyone knows what is meant, even if not everyone understands who the devil actually is."

"Yes ... o.k. ... that's an argument ... ... then I have another question: Buddha describes boundless composure as one of the four characteristics of an enlightened person, i.e. that a completely healed person can accept all events as they are. If I accept everything as it is, however, I also no longer have any preferences, i.e. there is also no longer any personal devil ... but I also just don't want anything anymore – so where are self-expression and self-fidelity?"

"You are not looking properly. To accept everything as it is and not to close your eyes to it means to be able to see the whole world – and, among other things, it also means that you have perfect telepathy. Seeing everything and accepting that it is the way it is in the here and now does not mean that you do not have a goal for your future – Buddha also had a goal: enlightenment for all! That is the essence of a Boddhisatva.

And of course Buddha also has a personal devil: He wants to end the suffering in the world – so his personal devil has the form of the collective devil. After all, this is shown very clearly in his writings: suffering is what Buddha fights against with all his might."

"Um ... you have, like all deities and also the souls, this amazing gift to argue simply, clearly and strikingly ... that is always impressive ..."

"As a deity, you are in the realm you like to call 'Da'ath' – there in this boundary-less realm of the gods you see everything ... that makes reasoning easy."

"Yes, I suppose that's true ... ... Is there anything more to say about 'Buddha and the Devil'?"

"No – if you don't want to hear a long-winded treatise on the history of religion ..."
"Can you do that too?"
"That would be my biography from your point of view ..."
"Yes, well ... I realize that ... ... but no thanks ... I don't think that would be really nutritious for me ....
Then thank you very much, devil!"
"You're welcome!"
"Ho!"

14. The Lustful God

The motif of reprocreation has linked death and sex – the two most emotionally charged themes of man, and therefore the two basic themes of the Scorpions.

Therefore it is no wonder that procreation has also been a highly emotionally charged theme. This has led to the herdanimal/human hybrid beings playing an important role in mythology: Fauns, Silenes, the Minotaur, the Stag Man, Freyr, etc.

It could not fail, of course, that these figures were also associated with earthly sex. Originally, Pan was the dead man in the afterlife who procreated with the afterlife goddess in goat form. Later, it became the lustful Pan, who chases the nymphs and has fun with them.

For Christianity, which was hostile to the body, the wild, lustful Pan was, of course, a figure of terror – he embodied the behavior that was not allowed to be. Consequently, Pan became a part of the devil – whereby the devil now and then also became a lustful figure.

In the Jugendstil period, i.e. around 1900, Pan became a popular motif that embodied, among other things, the dissolution of sexual blockades, new, freer and wilder forms of music and dance, and so on.

Later, Pan became the most important god in Wicca (witch cult), along with the goddess Isis.

The reprocreation also led to the telling of lewd jokes in the preparations for the Mysteries of Eleusis. This is also found in the myths of Demeter on which they are based, in which the maid Baubo makes the goddess Demeter laugh by erotic jokes and actions. This motif is further on found in other mysteries, as they were about a rebirth in this world, that is, a realization of one's soul in this world.

The rebirth has been further developed in yoga to the tantra yoga, which has the unification of the inner man with the inner woman as a goal, whereby also the own soul can be found, since the inner man and the inner woman are the two polar mirror images of the soul.

Another development is the ritual representation of this union. On the one hand, it existed as a special festival in which the Babylonian king united with the high priestess in the temple on the top of the step pyramid in order to give fertility to the land, and on the other hand, this unification ritual also existed as a ritual for everyone in the temples throughout the eastern Mediterranean area. This ritual is often rather misleadingly described with the term "temple prostitution", which completely ignores the religious basis of this ritual.

This varied sexual symbolism was of course a thorn in the side of the Christian church, so that they saw to it that all this symbolism was attributed to the devil – which in turn probably contributed to the church's hostility towards sexuality.

In the Middle Ages, one of the most important forms of the devil was the "sex devil", who gave people sexual desire, sexual fantasies and erotic dreams – whoever throws sexuality out the front door of his psyche, will be visited by it again in the form of the devil who comes through the back door …

A distinction was made between the succubus, which lay below – that is, the woman – and the incubus, which lay above – that is, the man.

This image of the devil began to dissolve in the Occident, first timidly with Jugendstil and finally quite thoroughly in the hippie era.

14th Dream Journey to the Devil

"Would you like to say something about that, devil?"

"Don't you have the saying, 'everything that's fun is fattening, immoral or illegal'? That's the dynamic: what you repress becomes what you crave most. You crave nothing more than to be able to live your personal devil. That which you repress is what you lack. And you have repressed your sexuality for centuries, so that it is what you lack the most. Fortunately, the hippies have largely put that right – they have collectively reintegrated that part of me, so that today most people can talk about sexuality in a reasonably relaxed way, and most people also do what they would like to do.

So the sex-devil is old news – at least to a large extent."

"Um ... every once in a while we do something right, don't we?"

"Now don't be so modest! You've already done quite a lot, even if there are still plenty of problems, of course. But you're beginning to realize that you have to do something."

"Yes ... and it is just the transition from an ending epoch to a new epoch, which is always quite exhausting ... and the materialism corresponds to the puberty of the individual and the now beginning globalization of the foundation of a family in the life of an individual ... And everyone who has ever founded a family knows what a change that is and that you first have to get together.

Yes, well ... I won't be so modest for once ... even though I tend to be ..."

"Yeah yeah ... that's your part of your personal devil ..."

"O.k. ... thank you, devil!"

"You're welcome."

"Ho!"

15. The Rebel

The fairly recent but widely known story of Lucifer's rebellion against God the Father is the basis for the concept of the devil as a rebel who revolts against the established order.

This motif has also been used by J.R.R. Tolkien at the beginning of his "Silmarillion", in which it is described how Ilúvatar ("Allfather") creates the world by music, but Melkor wants to create his own music and thus brings dissonance into Ilúvatar's music. Little by little, Melkor then develops into a kind of devil, whose servant is Sauron, who is the dark figure in "The Lord of the Rings" who wants to enslave Middle Earth.

Lucifer has thus become a role model for all those who feel constrained by the divine order, by the governments of states, or by the laws of nature, and who want to break through these barriers. Most clearly this rebellious (and scorpionic) basic attitude has been developed by the Gnostics to a complete world view and attitude towards life.

Satanism, too, lives to a large extent out of this rebellion against the existing order – especially, of course, against the Christian church. Since Satanism is largely limited to doing the opposite of what Christianity prescribes, Satanists do not move very far from Christianity, but are primarily an identification with the shadow of Christianity, i.e. an identification with the devil: "Sympathy for the Devil".

15th Dream Journey to the Devil

"Is this rebel role a central element with you, Devil?"

"No ... it was an explanation of the Middle Ages for the fact that I exist at all: a fallen angel. And it was also an unmistakable warning not to rebel against secular or spiritual authority. And in more recent times the Satanists and some others have identified themselves with me, because they see in me the rebel against the existing system. But I have not become the archetype of the rebel – look at 'Star Wars': there the 'good guys' are seen as rebels against the 'evil system', but the devil always remains 'the others' there too, so from the Yedi's point of view the Sith. The 'sympathy for the devil' is above all a good means to shock others ..."

"Um ... that's probably all there is on this subject, isn't it?"

"Yes."

"Thank you. ... ... Ho!"

16. The Collective Shadow

One can take the devil as the image of the collective shadow. This, of course, raises the question of what is the collective subconsciousness in which this collective shadow is located as an important image. And from that originates the question of what the conscious mind actually is.

Consciousness, in my opinion, is the inside of the world and matter is the outside of the world. There is only the one world, but it has two aspects.

A detailed account of this may be found in my book "The Synthesis of Physics and Magic".

The consciousness itself can cover different areas, i.e. have different contents – it also depends on it what kind of consciousness it is. There seem to be six kinds of consciousness:

The best known consciousness is the waking consciousness (which reads these very lines). It contains the information that is needed in the momentary situation to make meaningful decisions. These are "a few consciousness contents".

The waking consciousness is like a desk in an office, on which the informations needed at the moment lie.

The consciousness with the least content is ecstasy. It is the complete concentration on a single content – it is single-mindedness. It requires great motivation, which can be fear, pain, pleasure, meditative concentration, and a few other things.

The ecstasy consciousness can be thought of as the lamp on the desk in the office of the waking consciousness, brightly illuminating a single object.

The subconscious mind contains all perceptions and memories. They are arranged associatively, i.e. similar things as well as things experienced at the same time stand next to each other and form symbols, complexes and the personal mythology. The subconsciousness is perceived in dreams, on dream journeys and in premonitions. The waking consciousness can remember things in the archive or look at them on dream journeys – the office worker sends a messenger to the archive (memory) or goes to the archive himself (dream journey) to get a certain information.

The subconscious can be considered as the personal archive.

One reaches the <u>deep sleep consciousness</u> when one lets go of all consciousness contents and goes into the silence. This is consciousness itself without contents – the paper beneath the picture, and the silence behind the sounds.

One can consider the deep sleep consciousness as the house where the office and the archive are located.

The next consciousness, whose contents encompass an even larger area, is the <u>collective subconscious</u>. It can be reached and experienced in meditation or on dream journeys. In it all information about the world is accessible and there you can find the deities, the plant spirits, the spirits in the homeopathic pellets and similar "collective beings". There are also the information about previous lives and about the intention of the soul for its current incarnation.

The collective subconsciousness can be considered as the city in which the houses of different people are located. However, these houses are not isolated, but are connected with each other by paths, telephone lines, and the like. These links are the telepathy and the telekinesis. There are also general rhythms there, which one can grasp and also predict e.g. by astrology.

Finally there is the one, all-embracing consciousness, which one could call quite simply "<u>God</u>". In him the entire contents of the consciousness are not contained as single information as in the collective subconsciousness, but as unity.

This consciousness can be understood figuratively as the country in which the city stands.

The devil is a collective image and is therefore in the collective subconsciousness – after all, he is a deity, even if he is rarely referred to as such.

The images in the personal subconsciousness have connections to the archetypes in the collective subconsciousness – and the archetypes in the collective subconsciousness affect the images in the personal subconsciousness. This connection consists of telepathy – so the collective subconsciousness is not just a certain area of the brain where certain behavior patterns are stored in the DNA.

Of course, this description makes sense only if one has already experienced telepathy many times and thus assumes that it happens not only sometimes, but all the time.

Everything that has ever been thought, felt, meditated and experienced is stored in the collective subconsciousness. Moreover, the collective subconsciousness has telepathy as an "eye" and correspondingly telekinesis as a "hand". Finally, the devil is an image in this collective subconsciousness.

What does all this mean for the nature of the devil?

First of all, it means that the devil consists of a very large number of different kinds of images. It can be assumed that these images are ordered according to his development since his first beginnings in the Neolithic – thus in the form of the "biography of the devil".

Then this means that the devil can evolve through new images in people – e.g. the medieval repression and "demonization" of sexuality has been dissolved for the most part in the meantime. Of course, new images can also be added, such as the fear of the destruction of the entire humanity by the people themselves – through a nuclear war, global warming, the destruction of the environment, etc.

Finally one can also assume that the devil like all deities has telepathy and telekinesis and somewhat more inconspicuously also the "guidance of coincidence" as means of self-expression to his disposal. Here, of course, the question arises what motivations the devil has and what he wants to do – and whether he actually wants to do anything at all.

Generally the gods seem to intervene in the life of humans only if one asks them for it – in prayer, in conversation, on a dream journey, in an invocation or with an evocation etc. This should then actually also apply to the devil. Of course, there is also the "unconscious request": the fear of something summons what one is afraid of.

There is another point: All deities seem to know each other and to be something like "friends" – at least they are well-disposed to each other. I have experienced this so far on every dream journey and in every ritual and I have also not heard or read from others that they had experienced something different in the realm of the deities. Therefore, this should also apply to the devil. This follows already from the fact that the area of the deities is the "area without boundaries" – why telepathy and telekinesis are also normal there.

Now what results from these considerations for the nature of the devil? It seems to me to be simplest to ask the devil himself for this.

16th Dream Journey to the Devil

"What do you think of my considerations about you as an 'archetype in the collective subconsciousness'?"

"Sounds a bit bumpy formulated ... what do you think about the fact that I am a 'being with a body of life force'?"

"Sounds good ... Life force, in my opinion, is simply the boundary between consciousness and matter ... so you are an archetype, a collective content of consciousness – and consequently a life force being ... Um – that doesn't get me too much

further just yet ... Would you like to say something more about my thoughts on you in the last chapter?"

"What do you want to know?"

"Are you a friend of the other gods?"

"Yes – though 'friend' is a very human term ... We are qualitatively distinct parts in a continuum – endless different colored threads in the tapestry of the world, as it were. None of these threads can be missing – then the world would be incomplete."

"But these threads can form different patterns and motifs in the tapestry picture?"

"Yes."

"And we participate in their creation through our thoughts, our feelings, our will and our deeds?"

"Yes – especially through your deeds."

"Do you have the ability of telepathy and telekinesis and 'chance-guidance'?"

"Yes – we are talking to each other right now."

"Um – at that I can't perceive telepathy directly ... I just hear your voice in my head and then write that down."

"You've experienced enough to know that telepathy exists – and this is not the place to cite all the experiments that can be used to prove telepathy."

"Um ... I guess that's right ... I always want to make this as complete as possible ... yes, well ... ... Do you have a biography? I mean, is your history ordered in the collective subconsciousness like the memory of one's own biography in a human being? Is that comparable?"

"You can compare it that way – that's okay."

"But there are differences?"

"Yes."

"And they are not important here and belong in another book with another subject?"

"That's right."

"O.k. ... what about intervention? Are you acting on your own impulses?"

"Like attracts like. When someone thinks of me, I come to him. And I come in the way the person has thought of me. This is the general principle of magic: 'Like attracts like,' 'Like affects like,' 'Like and like join together,' 'Like is healed with like,' 'Like develops like,' etc. You could also say that I am in everything that is like me ....

But I am not the cause for it, if someone acts 'devilishly' – the cause for it lies in the person concerned, in his psyche, in his biography, in his world view, in his intentions etc..

I am an archetype, i.e. I have no body and consequently there are also no 'individual impulses' in me through which I manifest and express myself at a concrete point in the world. Instead I am a quality and I am present everywhere where this quality is. Always remember that I have no physical body and consequently have no impulses to bring about anything specific in the material world."

"I have the feeling that it is not so easy to understand what a deity is – and with you a lot of violent feelings are added, if one wants to look at you more closely ... ...

Then I still have a question, which belongs only very indirectly to the topic in this chapter:

I know how souls look when you perceive them directly – they usually have a human shape, they just stand there and smile silently, they have eyes of an indescribable depth (which you sometimes still see in newborns), they are colored and they sometimes glow from within.

How a deity looks, if one really perceives it and sees it not only on a dream journey in the usual dream journey way as slightly colored and as more or less shadowy or clear figure, I do not know very exactly – at least not as exactly as with the souls.

Well – the thing I want to know is what you look like when I see you as a deity."

"Look."

... ...

This is all very unexpected, what I perceive there ... my perception turns into me, i.e. inward – there is, so to speak, for me to see your beginning ... then an incredible love arises in me – like an expanding cloud, like a river, like an opening bud in the middle of my chest – there in the middle of my chest, where I have had cramps again and again for decades ....

This love expands ... it goes beyond my body ... this is more than love, this is ... a close cohesion ... this is almost identity ... no, not identity – 'cohesion' is more precise ... this is the quality of the astrological trine, the quality of the strong interaction which holds the three quarks together in the protons and neutrons, this is organic, indissoluble integration ...

Now this quality envelops me completely ... and goes beyond me ...

Do I see you now, devil, or ... do I see your effect on me?"

"You are integrating, you are beginning to show yourself, to open yourself. And you begin to become healed – that's what you've been striving for for two and a half years with your Kundalini meditations."

"That means that I have been missing you, devil, all this time – for me to become healed?"

"This is called 'integration of the shadow'."

"Um ... strangely enough, it never occurred to me to see and do that in such a literal and direct way. ... And you?"

"Stay with my effect in you – that's just the important thing."

"Yes ... you are actually right ... ... I am filling myself up from the inside out ... well, 'filling' is not quite right ... it is all growing back together in the right way ... it is falling into place again ... there are fissures, disturbances, dissonances being resolved ... ...

There is a spherical area in my chest where the integration seems to be completed ... the area is 40cm in diameter or something ... the center is in my heart chakra ... and the area has a pretty clear surface – it's spherical, yeah ... it goes further out, but there is a clear transition, it goes from one thing to another ... just like in the body it goes from bone to muscle, but the inside and the outside of this area belong together and are part of the same body ... ...

Is that it, devil? ... Or is there something else to see?"

"There is much more, but let it stand there for now – one step at a time ..."

"Thank you, thank you very much! ... ... Ho!"

17. The Individual Shadow

The devil is also the personal shadow – this is first of all the most important part of the devil …

As a rule, this will be a certain quality and ability that one has repressed and therefore not integrated. One can find this "personal devil" in many ways:

- In many cases, one will already know what one fears the most: War, separation, pain, aggression, hunger, cold, powerlessness, illness, lack, etc. In the vicinity of what one fears the most, one will also find the core of one's own shadow, which is usually an experience in a time long ago that has significantly shaped oneself.

- You can also look for painful repetitions in your own biography. It is quite certain that these repetitions are based on one's own shadow, one's own personal devil – which of course goes back to the same experience as in the previous point.

- There is also the possibility to have a closer look at one's own horoscope. It is almost always the square aspects that have caused the personal devil to arise. A square separates and can therefore also split off and suppress something, if one makes the mistake of considering only the planet on one side as "good" and the planet at the other end of the square aspect as "evil".

In some cases, the quincunxes, the semi-sextiles, or the isolated planets in one's chart can also be the point of origin for the personal devil, but usually it is the squares.

- At conception, the soul is reflected in the life force surrounding the fertilized ovum. This ovum is shaped from the matter side by the DNA in the egg and in the sperm, and from the consciousness side by the character of the soul and by its intention for its upcoming incarnation (which is shown, among other things, in the choice of its horoscope).

Since the life force is polar, the soul is reflected twice – once as a man and once as a woman. In a man this inner male image becomes the self-image and this inner female image becomes the search image – in a woman it is the other way round.

Now, if the person experiences something violent, it can happen that the psyche polarizes. When it comes to the topic "abundance", the addict and the ascetic are created, when it comes to the topic "strength", the perpetrator and

80

the victim are created, and when it comes to the topic "self-love", the star with the megalomania and the fan with the inferiority complex are created.

This polarization naturally also affects the inner male image and the inner female image, so that, for example, in the case of an abundance problem, an he-addict and an he-ascetic as well as an she-addict and an she-ascetic are created. Of these four images, the person concerned lives only one himself – e.g. the he-addict. The other three images are taken over by other people. The he-ascetic is the enemy of the he-addict, the she-addict is the friend of the he-addict and the she-ascetic is the relationship partner of the he-addict. Other he-addicts can possibly be his friends.

The whole results in the relationship mandala, which is then performed as the "life drama" of this he-addict and the people he is involved with.

This mandala shows that there are at least two personal devils: a male and a female, who have the same character. In the case of an he-addict, these are the he-ascetic as well as the female she-ascetic who, fatally, is also his relationship partner …

One cannot escape one's own shadow, i.e. the external creation of his two personal devils.

- The character of the soul and its intention for its forthcoming incarnation shape the life force body of the person concerned. Since there is the dynamic in the life force that like and like are layed together, the soul is joined by three allies for its present incarnation:

> - From the realm of animals, the animal joins the person concerned, which has the same dynamic as the person concerned: the spirit animal.

> - From the realm of plants, the plant joins the person concerned, which has the same attitude as the person concerned: the spirit plant.

> - From the realm of minerals, the mineral joins the person concerned, which has the same structure as the person concerned: the spirit stone.

If a polarization arises in the psyche of the person concerned through a violent experience, this polarization is also found in the three allies:

> If, for example, Mars is displaced, it may be that the wolf spirit animal is the last wolf in its pack in terms of rank – and somewhere a

81

tremendous aggression lies dormant.

In the case of a Mars blockade, the posture of the person concerned will probably be rather limp and powerless, and the stem or trunk of the power plant will sway excessively.

If there is a Mars problem, it will be also present in the formation of structure in the person concerned: these structures will be indecisive and not stable.

- Finally, there is the Kundalini, the awakening of which makes conscious and finally dissolves all blockages in the chakras. By the location of the main blockage in the chakra system, one can also see what the basic character of the personal devil is.

- blockage of the root chakra: ascetic
- blockade of the hara: victim
- blockade of the solar plexus: fan
- blockade of the throat chakra: ftar
- blockade of the third eye: perpetrator
- blockade of the crown chakra: addict

The radiance of the heart chakra is restricted by any major blockage within the chakra system.

The personal devil obviously has a differentiated character with many different aspects.

In connection with Kundalini there is another interesting connection: In homeopathy, sulfur (Sulphur) is prescribed when a patient has very unclear symptoms and it thus is not apparent what he is actually suffering from. With the help of sulfur you "light a fire under his butt", i.e. you stimulate his root chakra and thus also his Kundalini.

The well-known sulfur smell of the devil could thus be related to the root chakra and to the kundalini.

The lack of a great intensity of life, which is stimulated by the sulfur, is found extremely rarely in people with a Scorpio ascendant.

From these connections could also come the sympathy for the smell of sulfur in some Scorpios and likewise the sulfur smell of the devil – after all the devil seems to have a Scorpio ascendant … and a great intensity he has in any case.

17th Dream Journey to the Devil

"What would you like to tell me or show me next, devil?"
"Come with me."
"O.k. ... Where to?"
"Come."
"O.k."

I see a cartway ... it leads to a village ... it reminds me of the road from Klein-romstedt in Thuringia, where my father was born, to Großromstedt ... fields, fruit trees to the left and right of the paths ... we turn right and go down a very shallow slope ... below is a small brook, which flows from left/west to right/east – so back to Kleinromstedt ... I don't remember such a brook ... there are some pollard willows at the bank of the brook ... we sit down there at the bank in the grass ... I would like to lean to something, but at the place, where I sit, is no tree . . ... I just wait, what happens now ...

I see little fishes darting through the water of the brook ... the waves of the brook glisten in the sunlight ... I almost expect that now a emperor dragonfly will fly by and sit on my knee – as they often do when they want to tell me to just be in the here and now ...

I look to the left to the devil ... he now suddenly looks like Pan – actually I see him now for the first time really as a figure ... he whistles softly to himself ... I wrote a flute piece a few days ago – about how Pan sits at a brook and plays the flute and just is there and enjoys what is just ... you can listen to the flute piece at youtube under 'Eilenstein – Io Pan' ... this mood is now also here ...

There is nothing to do or to realize ... I lie down in the grass and listen to Pan ... listen to the splatter of the brook, the buzzing of the bees, the chirping of the birds ... now and then the wind rustles in the willows ...

I think I'll just sleep for a while here on the grass by the brook ... yes, that's what I'll do now ... see you later then ...

18. Devil and Trauma

A trauma is a component of the psyche that is in an extreme state: on the one hand, it is largely isolated from the rest of the psyche, and on the other hand, it is under the greatest possible pressure.

Even though a trauma can have very different contents, they all arise in the same way:

1. A person gets into a dangerous situation in which he faces his death, an extreme pain or similar. Here he has three possibilities:

> a) He sees a chance to avert the disaster and e.g. to kill the hungry lion. Then he will try that.

> b) He sees the possibility to escape the danger by a flight. Then he will try that.

> c) He sees no rescue possibility in attack or escape. Then he will give himself up.
> In such a situation the soul decides to leave the body because it sees no advantage in e.g. experiencing its body being eaten by a lion – the person faints.
> Therefore, this person experiences how he leaves his own physical body with his consciousness and with his ability of perception, hovers above it and observes the whole happening from a distance. This is then called "near-death experience" or "astral projection".
> In this way, people have discovered that man is more than just his body. Those who had such an experience and then learned to repeat such astral journeys at will were the first spiritual-magical specialists: the Shamans.

2. Now there are two possibilities how this situation can develop:

> a) This man really dies – then the story is over here (at least as far as his body and psyche are concerned – the soul continues to exist).

> b) This man survives, e.g. because his clan saved him – then the story continues.

3) After the rescue, the astral body of the person returns to his body and he wakes up from his faint. At this point the subject is still full of stress and the adrenaline level is at its maximum. There are three possible further develop-

ments here:

a) The subject begins to scream, shake, stomp, cry, etc., which relieves the stress and adrenaline. Then everything is okay again.

b) The person is prevented from this reduction of his stress by the people or the circumstances. Then he remains in the extreme state of stress.

c) The person is able to reduce his stress, but the dangerous situation repeats itself so often that he is no longer able to dissolve this stress by screaming, shaking, crying, raving, laughing, etc.

4. In the two cases in which the person is not able to relieve his stress (3.b and 3.c), the stress remains in him. The stress is confined and encapsulated so that the person can continue to live, but it still exists in the psyche. In this way, in the cellar of the psyche, so to speak, a tightly closed tin can with very intensive stress in it has been created, which is under great pressure. This tin can contains, above all, the image of the concrete danger of death (or the like) that one has experienced.

The content of this tin can, which is rattling away on the cellar shelf, naturally has an effect on the rest of the psyche. There are three possibilities here:

a) The person succeeds in isolating the trauma tin very thoroughly from the rest of the psyche. Then the subject can live a widely normal life. Only when he experiences something very similar to the fear-of-death image in the "tin can", the subject partially loses his contact with reality and begins to act as if he were back in the dangerous situation.

b) The subject manages to isolate the canned image of the trauma reasonably well from the rest of the psyche. Then the person can also live a normal life, but he is much more susceptible to a temporary loss of contact to reality – for this, a concrete situation only has to correspond reasonably exactly to the former danger situation. This can be difficult for the person.

c) The person hardly succeeds in isolating the canned image of the trauma from the rest of the psyche. In this case, the person has great difficulty in living a tolerably normal life. There are then very many and possibly in the course of time more and more possible triggers for losing contact to reality: Not only lions then cause the stress, but also all cats, then all animals, then everything that moves, etc. Then this person has a serious problem.

5. The healing of a trauma usually consists of several steps, where these steps can take very different amounts of time.

a) "Looking": The first step is the awareness that there is a problem and the willingness to look at it. One should proceed slowly and only look at as much as one can stomach.

In order to heal, one must know what the problem is. Every integration begins with looking at and getting to know what you want to integrate.

In this step and also in the two following steps it is very helpful to have a solid support from a friend, a therapist, a shaman, a deity or similar.

b) "Feeling": The second step is to feel in small amounts what is in the trauma. In doing so, one should always keep one's head above water and return to safe land when one begins to feel unsafe – sinking into the old fears does not help.

Either already when looking or now when feeling, one will see oneself in the dangerous situation – at the age one had at that time in that situation.

The friend, the therapist, the shaman or the deity who can give you support is very important here, because with their help you can go further than you could go alone. Moreover, these helpers can also appear in the danger image and drive away or kill the lion, for example.

c) "Embracing": The third step consists of the "today-me" embracing the younger "then-me", i.e. integrating it. Then the "then-me" can tremble, cry, laugh or rage to express and dissolve the stress trapped in the trauma.

This "defuses" the traumatic image of the danger-of-death situation. Afterwards, the person still has the memory of this experience (the "tin can" in his basement), but this tin can is no longer under pressure and is no longer full of stress: it is no longer an "extremely emotionally charged image" – the "tin can" is open and empty on the basement shelf, so to speak.

So what does trauma have to do with the devil? Well, there is nothing a person can fear as much as the contents of his trauma – after all, it is death-fear that is in the "trauma tin can". Trauma also makes a person inflexible, inelastic, and volatile and violent in unexpected ways. It is therefore quite easy to recognize a trauma by the fact that there are sore points in a person to which he reacts extremely violently and irrationally – so to speak "psychic contact mines" that explode immediately.

This can also be experienced in conversations when one unintentionally touches such a topic – the traumatized person then suddenly becomes angry, bursts into tears, becomes aggressive or simply leaves without any explanation and never comes back.

The trauma subject is feared like death – therefore the trauma (if there should be one in the psyche of a person) is the core of the personal devil.

Furthermore the trauma usually also has to do with a planet at one end of a square in the person's chart, it shows up as a blockage in a particular chakra, it shapes the state of the spirit animal, the spirit plant and the spirit stone – and sometimes it causes a blind spot in the person's memory when the trauma has been so well isolated that there is no contact from the rest of the psyche to that trauma anymore.

Therefore, it can also be said that people with a trauma are more prone to fear the devil – whatever the image of the devil is for them ... After all, some people fear most not the devil, but God, an orderly family life, travel to distant lands, diseases, or anything else of all possible things.

Thus, healing one's traumas also significantly reduces the fear of the personal devil – which in most cases will be quite similar to the collective devil.

18th Dream Journey to the Devil

"Would you like to say something about my thoughts regarding the connection between traumas and the devil?"

"Courage."

"Courage?"

"Yes, courage. You forgot to mention courage. To approach the healing of trauma requires courage. To heal the lion trauma, you have to go inwardly or outwardly to the lion that wanted to eat you and relive all the mortal fear you had then – and which you may only vaguely remember. It's so much more convenient not to resolve trauma and only half live because then half your psyche is blocked ... Look how long it took even you to come and see me – even though you've been working on self-healing for almost 50 years now."

"It just didn't occur to me to visit you ..."

"Yes – I had to appear to you first as the intuition to write this book."

"Er – does that mean that you do take initiative on your own and get involved in people's lives?"

"You called me by asking so intensely for healing. Only I could help you in the place where you are standing right now."

"Um, yes ... I understand that. ... So I had enough courage?"

"Yes ... otherwise I would not have come to you."

"I did come to you ..."

"You called me and I came – and you experienced this as a dream journey to me."

"Yes, o.k. ... that's how it was ... ... is there anything more to say about it?"

"Not for now."

"Thank you."

"You're welcome – and see you soon!"

"Yes, see you soon! ... ... Ho!"

19. Globalization

Since the Second World War it has become clear that we on earth need an overall coordination to prevent or reverse the wars, the atomic bomb, the environmental destruction, the global warming, the overpopulation, the extinction of species and the like more.

The destruction of the earth, i.e. more exactly the life possibility for humans on the earth, has become the new central element of the collective devil – thus what nobody wants. However, there are several problems connected with this:

- Not all people see this problem.

- Not all people are ready to solve it.

- Some people want others to solve it.

- Others insist on their egoism and care only for themselves.

- Then there are also the old "collective devils" such as xenophobia, the desire for power, individual and collective "short-sighted egoism".

The initial situation is not simple:

- There are currently different political systems – democracies, dictatorships, party dictatorships, extensive freedom of the individual, extensive control by an all-dominating party and many intermediate forms …

- There are also different economic systems – market economy, centrally planned economy, social market economy, tribal forms, dictatorships with unclear economic form, systems characterized by corruption …

- There are old enmities that have not really been resolved.

- There are, to put it very cautiously, reservations between the different races on earth.

- There is partly a massive mistrust between different religions.

- There is the claim of some religious extremists to world dominion.

- The raw materials are distributed very differently among the states.

These are not yet all problems – but at least the largest part of them. To bring this colorful mixture to a functioning cooperation is a mammoth task. On the individual level, this cooperation would correspond to the formation of a family in which the parents and the children are all completely different and no one really trusts the other.

The basic attitude necessary for this cooperation is the realization that each individual and each people needs the preservation of his or her individuality in order to be able to cooperate with the others, and that each individual and each people also needs to look at the whole in order to direct his or her own decisions and actions toward the functioning and flourishing of the whole.

This does not mean giving up one's own egoism, but it only means giving one's own egoism more level – what good is a new Porsche in the garage if there is no more water in the fields and consequently no more bread because of global warming? So instead of short-sighted egoism, far-sighted egoism is needed.

This does not mean at all that everyone has to be equal, that everyone has to have the same thing at his disposal and that there is a uniform culture – but it does mean that the differences must not be so great that they create greater tensions, and it means that no one must act in such a way that he harms the community as a whole.

To find such an attitude is already very demanding to quite difficult in a newly founded family – and to arrive at such an attitude and way of acting among the different peoples, economies, forms of government, religions etc. is about the most demanding thing one can imagine.

The "new devil" of the destruction of the habitability of the earth is the incentive to face the "old devils" of the fear of poverty, of foreigners, of the loss of identity, of the threat by others, of the fear of being robbed, of the military power of the neighboring state etc. and to dissolve them step by step. If we cannot cure our "old devils", our "new devil" will afflict us – then the earth will become uninhabitable … and the whole problem will be solved in this simple way.

What is needed is on the one hand the being carried by the whole, thus trust, and on the other hand the carrying of the whole, thus responsibility.

In the personal aewa, this is trust in the family and responsibility for the family.

In meditation, this is the attainment of the boundaryless state in which one meets the gods.

In psychology, this is the realization of the collective subconsciousness – and precisely the integration of all the old devils that are in this collective subconsciousness as archetypes. This is necessary, because otherwise the old devils prevent us from solving the real actual problems, which can otherwise become a new devil, which we see not only as the undesirable possibility of the self-destruction of the people on Earth, but which will then become our very concrete reality – precisely our self-destruction.

19th Dream Journey to the Devil

"What do you think of my reflections, devil? Do I see it correctly? Does the image of the old devils and the new devil make sense?"

"The image is meaningful if it helps you to behave sensibly. ... Or if it helps others to behave sensibly."

"Um ... can you say more about that? I don't know if I've gotten to the bottom of that yet ..."

"That's all right – what you're doing right now is your part in this collective transformation."

"Um ... any more tips?"

"The new image of the devil is, after all, becoming increasingly clear in recent years, and it's also being spoken louder about – and rather tentatively, people are starting to behave differently, after all."

"Um ... well ... ... Thank you very much, devil!"

"You're welcome."

"Ho!"

20. Fool and Devil

The devil appears mainly in the monotheistic religions, where he is what God and the king do not want.

In the tribal religions, which are characterized by magic and mythology, another figure is found instead of the devil: the fool.

This fool is also known as the "trickster." He can take quite different forms. What all variants of the trickster have in common is that he does things wrong and therefore fails. By doing so, he ultimately proves that it makes sense to follow the rightness – simply because then you succeed.

- The heyoka (Dakota language: fool, inverted, opposite) is a man among the North American prairie Indians who does everything the other way around: "yes" means "no" to him, he sits on the horse looking backwards, he is gay, he sleeps by day, he drinks water from a gourd with holes in it, etc.

You become a heyoka when you dream of thunder – if you dream of lightning, you become a shaman. The shaman shows people the rightness, the Heyoka shows people the wrongness. The shaman teaches people by leading them to deeper insights – the heyoka teaches people by making them laugh.

- The trickster is someone who wants to outsmart others, but who in the end always falls into the pit he has dug for others. The trickster, unlike the heyoka, is a mythological figure, meaning that stories are told about the trickster's wiles and follies.

- In many North American stories, the coyote is the trickster. He tries to catch and eat different animals, but with all his tricks he usually only harms himself.

- The only European near equivalent to the coyote trickster are the stories about the fox and the wolf, where the fox is the cunning one and the wolf is the dolt. Unlike the trickster, however, the fox is usually successful, but at least the "dumb" wolf also involuntarily keeps portraying how not to do it.

- In Dakota mythology, the spider-man Iktomi is the inventor of most of the things people use. He is also considered by the Dakota to be the inventor of the Internet, among other things. Iktomi spins his lists like his spider webs, but in the end almost always gets caught in them himself.

- Spider webs have also led to the motif of the spider-man in West Africa, where he is called "Anansi". He is also a trickster, but in contrast to his relative Iktomi in the Dakotas, he is often victorious over stronger opponents and is more like the fox in Europe.

- The most famous trickster in the European mythologies is Loki – he always tries to outwit the Aesir in general and the thunder god Thor in particular, but is almost always defeated by Thor due to his physical strength.

- The Mahasiddhas, who were a Buddhist yoga movement in northern India around 1000 A.D., also have traits of tricksters, as they use people's weaknesses to help them reach enlightenment. Thus, a glutton is given a meditation in which he meditates only on food, a musician is said to meditate on the silence behind all sounds, and a power-hungry robber is given a meditation by which he becomes both omnipotent and enlightened ... This approach is called "removing water in the ear with water."

- The jesters at the medieval courts had a similar function as the Heyoka. They were the only ones who were allowed to give their opinion to the king and who exposed people's mistakes in a humorous to drastic way. A good court jester could achieve a great deal by his actions, as he made people aware of their own actions and the consequences of these actions. He had the task of waking people up and getting them out of their unconscious and reflex-like actions.

- Unfortunately, today's clown has little in common with the trickster and the jester. Only the hospital clown, whose main purpose is to cheer up children and long-term patients, still has a bit of a therapeutic function.

The Trickster is an alternative to the Devil: the Devil is the feared and the unwanted in royalty and monotheism – and the Trickster shows the unwanted in a friendly way in tribal cultures. The devil has the harshness of the hierarchy of kingship and monotheism – the trickster has the laughter of the self-knowledge of the self-determination in the tribal organization.

20th Dream Journey to the Devil

"Hello devil, how do you see your relationship with the 'wise fool' and the Trickster?"

"Nice contemporaries – at least they know that I exist, but are not afraid of me. You can talk to them ..."

"Is there anyone who is particularly sympathetic or familiar or close to you?"

"You should only ask questions where you're really looking for the answer, Harry."

"Um ... yes ... actually I don't have any questions regarding 'Fool and Devil' ... I was just hoping you might know something else that might be important ..."

"Then ask me exactly that too! So you want to know something that is important for you?"

"Yes – that is, for me or for the readers of this book or for people in general."

"O.k. – to the readers of this book: If you read this book and then don't change anything in your life, you might as well have left it alone – waste of time! So come and visit me yourself – then we'll talk."

"Um ... is there anything else to say in general, perhaps?"

"Hey! Ask if you really have a question and not just to fill your book!"

"O.k., o.k. ... I think I got it ... So, I don't have a question for you right now."

"Good – then I want to tell you something. ... Go with your attention to your hara."

"O.k. ... ."

"Describe it."

"Hm ... four finger widths below my navel ... indistinctly perceptible ... the connection from the root chakra to the hara has become clearer through my meditations in the last weeks ... I can perceive it ..."

"Go into your hara properly."

"O.k. ... I do ... ... I set my PC to 'record' and then close my eyes and speak out loud everything I see and do and record it ... ... I go down from my head ... through my oral cavity, through my throat ... chest ... abdomen ... ...

Hmm, it's difficult to get to the hara – there's something that keeps me away from it."

"Look at it."

"It's spherical – so the obstacle ... ... I can go left and right of it, in front of it and ... behind it ... and under it – no problem ... hm ... Indeed! ... I've never seen anything like this before ... er ... What is this? ... It's firm, but not hard, it's like a ... shell ... a shell, but ... it's a little bit paper-like, but organic, but not as dry-crumpled as paper ... I'll rub my hand over it ... ...

I wish I could go in there... ... ... um – I suddenly see the attic room at my parents', where I lived for a long time... And what is actually here? ... yes ... it feels a bit empty and uninhabited, my hara ... How is the connection from the hara downwards? ... What does it look like? ... It's clogged, it's a hose ... I'll clean it ... ... I've got a whole bucket full of dirt – the hose is free now ... And the connection upwards? ... It's also like a hose, but ... that's ... like cobwebs ... so ... that's different stuff than downstairs ... I'll get that out too ... I'll put it in another bucket ... that makes more of an impression like being unused and not like being blocked ... ...

There's a fear of letting the life force flow into the hara ... o.k. – I get a kind of twinge on the right side of my chest ..."

"Now stay down there."

"What's there? ... What's going on there? ... Now what am I supposed to do with the dirt in those two buckets?"

"Make a fire."

"Make a fire? ... All right ... I'll light this ... the stuff in the bucket with the stuff from the solar plexus burns really fast ... and the other one ... is a bit like damp coal ... it glows away ... well, now it's really igniting! ... I'll put it so that the fire goes upwards ... or should that be in the root chakra? ... no ... this is already right here in the hara ... o.k. ... that feels good ...

Probably this stuff are coals, i.e. the energy that actually wanted to rise, but then got stuck and then solidified, so to speak – then the burning fits to it ...

Well ... What is here in the center of the hara? ... hm, somehow nothing ... yes, yes, there is something, but ... nothing intact ... ... um – I would have expected you here now, devil, or something like that ..."

"Call the picture that's there, so you can see it."

"Oh ... yes ... a little Harry getting beaten up ... sure – that fits a switched off hara, yes ... ... I take little Harry in my arms ... he's shaking ... ...

The center of the hara is starting to get color ... red ... with a hint of orange ...

That was ... mainly the beating of my father ... that surprises me now ... I thought the beating of my mother would have bothered me more ... anyway ... ... There is my she-wolf, my spirit animal! ... She sniffs at my Hara ... she likes that, she likes that something happens ... ... let's see ... um ... my Thuja is also getting stronger ... my spirit plant ... um ... and the rock crystal? ... ... it seems to have been more of a help to get here ... ok. ... ...

Should I make the connection down to the earth's core, devil?'

... ...

"Just a little bit. ... ... That can really get going during your next meditation."

"There's still this coal in the bucket that's glowing ... I'm getting a feeling for how it might feel when a hara really gets going ... ... um ... Do you need something, hara? ... Doesn't seem so... And you, little Harry? ... He's also happy on my arm ... O.k. – and what do you think, devil?"

... ...

"I have shown you where your devil is – in the hara, there is your blockade ... hara-blockade, Mars-blockade ... no firm stand of your own ..."

"Yes ... whereas ... I'm surprised that I didn't see the devil there ..."

"The coal, Harry!"

"Um ... yes ... that's right ... the devil doesn't always have to have two horns ... the burning of the coal is now the devil's redemption, so to speak?"

"You could call it that."

"Yes, well ... then ... I'll leave it that way now ..."

The devil nods ...

"Yes, well – then I return now back again ... from this dream journey to my hara back into my head ... I see my hara now so to speak still from above ... then I open my eyes again ...

Yes ... thank you very much, dear devil! ... You really always have a surprise for me ..."

"Yes – that's the thing about the repressed ... you just don't know it so well ..."

"Um ... logical ... yes ... O.k.! ... Yes – thank you! ... See you soon!"

"See you soon!"

"Ho!"

21.   The Devil in the Four Elements

The essence of the devil depends on the point of view of the observer, because the devil is the unwanted. It also happens that for some people the existing order is the unwanted and therefore the devil represents the wanted.

This situation makes it difficult to describe not only the religious-historical collective devil but also the personal views about the devil – these views are simply too manifold. In order to get at least a little closer to these many possibilities, one can consider these possibilities with the help of some grids. Probably the simplest of these grids are the four elements.

Fire is first of all strength, expansion and therefore also powerful movement and secondly also fight, sexuality and ecstasy and as essence power.

From the point of view of the element fire a devil could be dominant, cruel, egocentric, ruthless and sadistic on the one hand, but on the other hand also submissive, unstable, listless and masochistic.

In general, a "fire devil" would be the image of "not being in one's own power". However, this can be seen quite differently: not being the strongest, not rebelling successfully or not defeating the rebels … In the end, the question here is always a fight and who wins it – this results in the image of the devil shaped by the element fire.

Water is first of all feelings, sympathy, antipathy, sympathy and as essence love.

From the point of view of the element water, a devil could thus be whiny, excessively altruistic, melting person, but also emotionless, inconsiderate and contact-lacking person.

In general, a "water devil" would be the image of the "emotional imbalance", whereby this can be both a too much of feelings, i.e. being flooded by feelings, and a too little of feelings, i.e. an emotional drought … In the end, it is always about feelings and needs and about who achieves their fulfillment and how – this results in the image of the devil, which is characterized by the element water.

Air is first of all thinking, speaking, arguing, logic, knowledge and as essence truth.

From the point of view of the element air a devil could therefore think too little, be unclear, confused and forgetful, but also too much thinking, being a liar, agitator, polemicist and hair-splitter.

In general, an "air devil" would be the image of "thinking out of balance", whereby there is both the too little of the dull stupor and the too much of the pedantic grumbler … The question here is ultimately always the knowledge, but often also the question of who can assert himself with his words against others - from this arises the image of the devil, which is shaped by the element air.

Earth is first of all firmness, constancy, nourishment, foundation, solid form and as essence thriving.

From the perspective of the element earth, a devil could thus be poor, renouncing and fickle, but also greedy, hoarding, clinging and dogged.

In general, an "earth devil" would be the image of "not giving", whereby there is here both the too great firmness and fertility as well as the too little firmness and fertility … The question here is ultimately always whether one finds the right measure of demarcation, possession and enjoyment or not – this results in the image of the devil shaped by the element earth.

Perhaps one should rather call these considerations "shadow sides of the four elements", but since these shadow sides are what the character of the devil consists of, one can also regard these considerations as "character studies of different manifestations of the devil".

Here, of course, no new form of the devil's hierarchy is intended to be sketched out – this consideration serves only to illustrate the various possibilities of what can be the essence of the devil for a certain person.

21ᵗʰ Dream Journey to the Devil

"Hello devil – do you find this kind of contemplation helpful and meaningful?"
"They are your way of approaching things – that's enough, isn't it?"
"Um … in a very personal way, yes … But do you have the impression that it makes it clearer what the essence of the devil is?"
"The scholastics have already investigated this – so you find yourself in sufficiently pedantic company …"
"Is that irony now?"
"Yes, of course!"
"You think it's too pedantic?"
"No – not at all … I'm just giving a broad hint to you: you're falling prey to the temptations of an air devil right now by losing sight of the right amount of detail."

"Um ... well ... then this is now helpful for the readers in several respects ... as a consideration of the four elements and their shadow sides and also about at how many places a devil can lurk.

Um ... it might be important that one determines oneself, which measure one finds correct and corresponding to oneself with which topic – right?"

"If you don't do things in your own style, you are not being true to yourself. The point is to go your own way – deviation from it is the unwanted and consequently the personal devil. The general view of what should be and what should not be is of importance only because it shapes the environment in which you live.

First it's about the 'ego-devil' and only then about the 'superego-devil', to develop Freud's terms further."

"Um ... well ... then I will now write two more chapters, which tend to go into a bit too much detail ... but which hopefully will be helpful for one or the other.

Merci vielmals!"

"Bittschön."

"Ho!"

22. The Devil in the Ten Planets

The seven classical planets that can be seen with the naked eye have been the basis for the seven deadly sins – which, of course, are what the devil wants to tempt people to do from the Christian point of view. Since the seven deadly sins correspond only approximately to the shadow sides of the astrological characteristics of the planets, here follows a consideration of the shadow sides of the ten planets from an astrological point of view.

The shadow or the devil is either a "too much" and "too loud" of something or a "too little" and "too quiet" of something. Of course, the degree perceived as correct varies greatly from individual to individual.

Moon
> Qualities: contact, sympathy, perception, sensation, helpfulness, intimacy
> Too-much shadow: mothering, inability to concentrate, clinging, addiction, to please others, dependence
> Too-little shadow: apathy, flatness, isolation, asceticism, need of help

Mercury
> Qualities: intellect, thinking, speaking, clarity, logic, conclusiveness, science
> Too-much shadow: pedantry, hair-splitting, stubbornness, inflexibility, self-opinionatedness
> Too-little shadow: inaccuracy, stupidity, illogic, sloppiness

Venus
> Qualities: sympathy, antipathy, affection, dislike, sense of beauty, love
> Too-much shadow: vanity, addiction to harmony, nymphomania, needing all attention
> Too-little shadow: neglect, ugliness, disharmony, gray mouse

Sun

Characteristics: self-love, egocentricity, resting in oneself, self-expression, radiance

Too-much shadow: excessive egocentricity, megalomania, lounge lizard, star, needing all the applause, needing to be the center of everything.

Too-little shadow: lack of egoism, inferiority complex, fan

Mars

Characteristics: strength, assertiveness, courage, willingness to take risks, fight, sex, competition

Too-much shadow: sex addiction, cruelty, will to destroy, sadism, Springinsfeld

Too-little shadow: repressed sexuality, fearfulness, timidity, masochism

Jupiter

Characteristics: goals, ideals, building, management, thriving, enjoying, cooperation

Too-much shadow: gluttony, self-overload, imperiousness, doggedness, inflexibility

Too-little shadow: Lack of drive, lack of goals, lack of energy, resignation

Saturn

Characteristics: firmness, security, foundation, constancy, preservation, protection.

Too-much shadow: hardness, stiffness, principled, suppression, stubbornness.

Too-little shadow: insecurity, fickleness, conformity, changeability, lack of foundation.

Uranus

Characteristics: inventiveness, new things, inventions, new contexts, new forms, new possibilities

Too-much shadow: uncontrollability, jumpiness, losing the thread, confusion

Too-little shadow: lack of ideas, lack of intuition, no perspectives, boredom

<u>Neptune</u>

    <u>Qualities</u>: imagination, art, religion, meditation, ecology, spirituality, social commitment

        <u>Too-much shadow</u>: dissipation, unsustainability, illusions, fantasy, self-sacrifice

        <u>Too-little shadow</u>: isolation, lack of imagination, lack of basic trust, environmental degradation

<u>Pluto</u>

    <u>Qualities</u>: single-mindedness, essentiality, commitment, ecstasy, intensity

        <u>Too-much shadow</u>: doggedness, fixation, blinkered mentality, ruthlessness

        <u>Too-little shadow</u>: laxness, lack of depth, absent-mindedness, superficiality.

From this short overview one can see how various forms the personal shadow can have and how variously therefore also the shadow of a people, i.e. the devil figure in the culture concerned can be described.

22th Dream Journey to the Devil

"Hello devil – what is the most essential thing you can tell me right now? ... Or better yet, what is the most essential thing you can tell me for this book, i.e. for its readers?"

"You write the book! Don't try to use me for your purposes! If you have a question yourself, then I will answer it for you – or not. But I can't stand these searches for essentials."

"Um ... is that part of my shadow?"

"Well – at least your mind works."

"Searching for depth where there is none right now?"

"I think, Harry, I need to revise what I just told you about your mind."

"O.k. ... So I'm looking for more intensity than I have in my life right now ... did I get that right now?"

"You must know that ... But I find that you are closer to the essential now."

"Um ... is that because of my Pluto/Saturn square?"

"It's not because of that – that describes that."

"Yes, well – that's more precise."

"It's not just a question of wording, it's a question of whether you're really taking responsibility for your life!"

"O.k. ... can you give me a tip on that?"

"Don't write so much – go out hiking, improvise music, dance, visit other people ... then you will get closer to what you are actually looking for."

"Yes ... ... Thank you."

"You're welcome."

"Ho!"

23. The Devil in the Twelve Signs of the Zodiac

The same thing that can be done with the ten planets can be done also with the twelve signs of the zodiac – that is, looking at the basic styles of the signs of the zodiac together with their two possible deviations, that is, their distortion to two opposite extremes.

Aries
> Characteristics: direct, spontaneous, simple, powerful, in the here and now, impetuous
>> Too-much shadow: hasty, erratic, choleric, careless, not prudent
>> Too-little shadow: hesitant, lacking drive, doubtful, not enthusiastic

Taurus
> Characteristics: to collect, to protect, to care, to store, to enjoy, to prosper
>> Too-much shadow: stingy, hoarding, greedy, constricting, robbing, caring to death, leaving no free space
>> Too-little shadow: to let go to waste, to live in want, not to protect, to be unloving

Gemini
> Qualities: curious, enterprising, inventive, nimble, humor
>> Too-much shadow: restless, unfocused, confused, unable to finish anything
>> Too-little shadow: unimaginative, dull, uninterested, listless

Cancer
> Characteristics: sensitive, introverted, protective, nurturing, warming, seeking contact
>> Too-much shadow: mothering, overprotective, constricting, clinging to someone, overemotional
>> Too-little shadow: insensitive, careless, apathetic, insensitive

Leo

Qualities: self-centered, strong-willed, radiant, creative, shaping

Too-much shadow: egocentric, megalomania. show-off, always has to be the center of attention

Too-little shadow: self-doubt, fan, inferiority complex, shy

Virgo

Characteristics: careful, accurate, cautious, planning, attention to detail, sensitive, prone to disturbances

Too-much shadow: oversensitive, easily irritated, pedantic, obsessive about order, compulsive about control

Too-little shadow: careless, negligent, imprecise, wanton, chaotic, untidy

Libra

Characteristics: beauty, harmony, balance, diplomacy, connection, relationships

Too-much shadow: addiction to harmony, making things look more beautiful than they are, conforming, spineless

Too-little shadow: letting things go to waste, lack of contact, lack of interest

Scorpio

Characteristics: getting to the point, intensity, depth, relationship, single-mindedness

Too-much shadow: biting, destructive, aggressive, extreme, inconsiderate

Too-little shadow: lax, no depth, listless, chaotic-emotional

Sagittarius

Characteristics: idealistic, determined, always ready, enthusiastic, ready for action

Too-much shadow: over-excited, hyperactive, constantly setting new goals, overtaxing oneself.

Too-little shadow: listless, no goals, resigned, powerless, apathetic

Capricorn

    Characteristics: thorough, certainty, foundation, realistic, matter-of-fact

        Too-much shadow: authority-believing, existential fear, stickler for principle, emotionally cold

        Too-little shadow: disoriented, no foundation, unobjective, fickle

Aquarius

    Characteristics: farsighted, smart, inventive, quick comprehension, generalizing, looking for basics, utopias, community of like-minded people

        Too-much shadow: overexcited, erratic, lives in cloud-cuckoo-land, can't bring anything down to earth, loss of reality

        Too-little shadow: lack of ideas, resignation, no vision for the future, lack of contact

Pisces

    Characteristics: sensitive, hunches, intuitive, sensitive, sympathetic, helpful

        Too-much shadow: disoriented, self-sacrificing, can't get down to earth, live in a dream world, drugs, fogged up

        Too-few shadows: insensitive, needy, disoriented, unimaginative.

This list is also mainly intended to show how many different qualities the personal shadow and thus the personal devil may have.

23ᵗʰ Dream Journey to the Devil

"Hello devil ... I have asked you so many questions by now that I am beginning to run out of questions."

"Then stop asking! Do you have to add a dream journey to every chapter? That's part of your shadow: excessive order and completeness."

"Er ... o.k. ... yes, well ... That means I have an order devil in me that could use a little more space and freedom?"

"Yes ... your ability to organize things systematically is good ... but don't overdo it ..."

"Yes ... well ... then first of all thank you for your hint!"

"You're welcome."

"Ho!"

24. The Devil and the Qliphoth

In Jewish mysticism, the Tree of Life is the central symbol. It represents the world as an organic structure that is at once unity and multiplicity, that is, God and the world. The structure of this Tree of Life can be found in everything from the structure of a vacuum cleaner to the structure of a cell to the basic structure of a state – but the detailed presentation of these possibilities would take too much space in this book (if needed, see my books "Blossoms of the Tree of Life I, II, III").

The Kabbalistic Tree of Life is basically a very simple structure:

> - Its basic principle is unity as the starting point and multiplicity as the result, and in between a developmental step or differentiation of unity to multiplicity.

> - The middle step of this "three-step" (the developmental step) is differentiated once again into three steps – this creates the five areas on the Tree of Life, also called the "Middle Pillar". They are separated from each other by the four transitions.

> - Finally, these three middle steps are then subdivided once again into three steps each. In this way a differentiated, eleven-part development structure results.

The Derivation of the Kabbalistic Tree of Life I					
Herleitung			*Sephiroth* *(areas)*	*Planet* *(assignments)*	*Tree of Life* *(graphic)*
I	*II*	*III*			
1.	1.	1.	Kether	Pluto	
2.	2.	2.	Chokmah	Neptune	
		3.	Binah	Uranus	
		D	Da'ath	Saturn	
	3.	4.	Chesed	Jupiter	
		5.	Geburah	Mars	
		6.	Tiphareth	Sun	
	4.	7.	Netzach	Venus	
		8.	Hod	Merkury	
		9.	Yesod	Moon	
3.	5.	10.	Malkuth	Earth	

The derivation of the Tree of Life graph can also be represented as follows:

The Derivation of the Kabbalistic Tree of Life II				
1. a system	2. the first diffe-rentiation into the three phases "Origin, Deve-lopment, Goal".	3. the second differentiation of the middle phase into three sub-phases each	4. the third diffe-rentiation of the three sub-phases into three sub-sub-phases each	5. the traditional representation of these eleven spheres as a Tree of Life.

The eleven spheres (circles, areas) on this graph are called "Sephiroth", which simply means "numbers" – these areas on the Tree of Life have obviously always been numbered for clarity.

The eleven Qliphoth are the "negative Sephiroth", so to speak. Their name means "husk, shell, pod" – the Qliphoth are like the shell of a fruit or a nut, which protects the core. So the Qliphoth will have originally meant that which shrouded the core of the Sephiroth, or the Sephiroth itself.

The Qliphoth cover God, so that the human being cannot recognize him immediately. This conception corresponds to the illusion "Maya" in Hindhuism, the devil Mara in Buddhism and the sin in Christianity.

In the early descriptions of the Qliphoth, there were only four sheaths around the innermost, that is, around God himself. The concept of ten Qliphoth enveloping each of the eleven Sephiroth came much later. Only 10 Qliphoth and not eleven are cited because the Sephirah Da'ath was considered invisible, representing the destroyed connection between this world and the hereafter, between the world and paradise, and thus generally between God and man. It was by this destruction, in Christian terms therefore by the Fall of Man, that the Qliphoth came into being in the first place as a veiling of the divine original state.

However, there was also a dual conception in Jewish mysticism in which God created good and evil.

Interestingly, in the older writings, evil (i.e., the Qliphoth) is seen as an emanation of the fifth Sephirah Geburah. This is the sphere of Mars, that is, the realm of power, aggression, struggle, transformation, sexuality, karma, etc. The archangel of the Sephirah Geburah is Samael, who later became Satan.

This shows that aggression and sexuality and transformation have been considered the central qualities of the devil – which fits well with most traditional depictions of the devil in the monotheistic religions.

Samael is the archangel of the Sephirah Geburah, which is the realm of karma and purgatory. Samael, or later Satan, is also the accuser in the afterlife court, which is the Mediterranean equivalent of the karma principle in India: both are to restore justice.

In another place in the Kabbalistic writings it is said that no Sephirah resembles God as much as Geburah – thus Samael is the archangel who is most like God. Samael restores justice and divine order by his accusations and his punishments.

Depending on the worldview, the relationship between the Sephiroth and the Qliphoth can be understood quite differently:

- The Sephiroth as the holy state and the Qliphoth as the sick state – then the sick state hides the holy state hidden in it.

- The Sephiroth as the ideal and the Qliphoth as the fear – then the Qliphoth are the shadow of the Sephiroth.

- The Sephiroth and the Qliphoth as two equal opposites – then they would be God and Devil in a dualistic world view.

- The Sephiroth as the good and the Sephiroth as the evil – then they would be mainly an evaluation.

Now you can choose which interpretation you prefer: the healing approach (version 1), the psychological approach (version 2), the scorpionic approach (version 3) or the monotheistic approach (version 4). There are, of course, still more ways to interpret the relationship between the Sephiroth and the Qliphoth.

It is obvious to take a closer look at the qualities of each Sephiroth and Qliphoth:

Sephiroth and Qliphoth	
Sephiroth	*Qliphoth*
1. Kether ("crown") - Name: Eheieh - Planet: Pluto	1. Thaumiel ("God's twin") - Name: Satan, Moloch - Planet: Pluto
2. Chokmah ("wisdom") - Name: Jah - Planet: Neptune	2. Ghagiel ("confusion of God's power") - Name: Beelzebub, Adam Belial - Planet: Neptune
3. Binah ("Insight") - Name: YHVH Elohim - Planet: Uranus	3. Sathariel ("concealment of God") - Name: Lucifuge Rofocale - Planet: Uranus
-. Da'ath ("hnowledge") - Name: YHVH - Planet: Saturn	-
4. Chesed ("grace") - Name: Jah - Planet: Jupiter	4. Gha'agsheblah ("man-eater") - Name: Astaroth (=Ishtar, Isis) - Planet: Jupiter
5. Geburah ("strength") - Name: Elohim Gibor - Planet: Mars	5. Golachab ("the all-burning") - Name: Asmodaeus - Planet: Mars
6. Tiphareth ("beauty") - Name: YHVH Eloah va-Da'ath - Planet: Sun	6. Thagirion ("those who cause sorrow") - Name: Belphegor - Planet: Sun
7. Netzach ("victory") - Name: YHVH Tzabaoth - Planet: Venus	7. A'arab Zaraq ("ravens of the burning of God") - Name: Ba'al, Tubal Cain - Planet: Venus
8. Hod ("shine") - Name: Elohim Tzabaoth - Planet: Mercury	8. Samael ("God's desolation") - Name: Adramelech - Planet: Mercury
9. Yesod („foundation") - Name: Shaddai el-Chai - Planet: Mond	9. Gamaliel ("God's defilement") - Name: Lilith - Planet: Moon
10. Malkuth ("kingdom") - Name: Adonai ha-Aretz - Planet: Earth	10. Nehemoth ("night ghosts") - Name: Nehema - Planet: Earth

Once aside from the fact that these 10 Qliphoth are a fairly new concept, there is little more information about them than their names, which merely indicate that they are the shadow sides of the Sephiroth. Thus, looking at the Qliphoth does not help much in exploring the nature of the devil …

Of course, one can also deduce the essence of the Qliphoth from the essence of the Sephiroth as their disturbance. That would be:

- Sephiroth Kether: Unity
- disturbance (Qliphoth Thaumiel): non-recognition of unity

- Sephiroth Chokmah: unhindered self-expression
- disturbance (Qliphoth Ghagiel): impeded self-expression

- Sephiroth Binah: community
- disturbance (Qliphoth Sathariel): isolation

- Sephiroth Da'ath: continuum
- disturbance (Qliphoth): fear of dissolving one's own boundaries

- Sephiroth Chesed: overall organization
- disturbance (Qliphoth Gha'agsheblah): disorder in the organization

- Sephiroth Geburah: power
- disturbance (Qliphoth Golachab): violence

- Sephiroth Tiphareth: identity
- disturbance (Qliphoth Thagirion): self-uncertainty

- Sephiroth Netzach: feeling
- disturbance (Qliphoth A'arab Zaraq): emotional blockades

- Sephiroth Hod: cognition
- disturbance (Qliphoth Samael): errors

- Sephiroth Yesod: Life force
- disturbance (Qliphoth Gamaliel): traumas

- Sephiroth Malkuth: Body
- disturbance (Qliphoth Nehemoth): disease

The qualities of the Qliphoth in this overview correspond to the qualities of the devil, which have already been mentioned in earlier considerations.

24th Dream Journey to the Devil

"Do you think, devil, that I have understood the Qliphoth? Or is there still something important missing?"

"If you are a systematization freak, then the Qliphoth are helpful – otherwise it makes far more sense to start with yourself and ask yourself what your personal devil is, what your shadow is – or what the collective devil, the collective shadow is."

"Yes ... that makes sense ... ... So – can you tell me something else about the collective shadow?"

"Act differently than your fear tells you – act the way your heart tells you."

"Hm ... yes ... courage is often needed for the 'way of the heart' ... and courage belongs to Mars and Mars is the Sephirah Geburah and Geburah is the realm of purgatory, karma, transformations ... and the home of the Archangel Samael, who then became Satan ... so you need courage because you are afraid of the devil ...

And why is it said in the Sepher Yezirah that Geburah is most similar to the essence of Kether, that is, unity?"

"Geburah is the doing, the transformation – that's what you're in the world with. That's where something happens. That's where things change. That's where you're really fully in the here and now."

"As Goethe says, 'In the beginning was the deed.' ... or as Heraclitus put it: 'War is the father of all things.' ... Is the devil thus indeed above all a Mars demon?"

"If Geburah is the most perfect expression of the unity of Kether, then the Geburah devil must also be the 'most perfect expression of the devil,' that is, the most important and influential and therefore the most famous devil ... and what is worse than violence, murder, rape, war and such things more? ... or in the hereafter then the experience of karma or purgatory – that is, the two variants of the judgment of the hereafter?"

"Then the Mars Devil has been so threatening to me not only because I have had a Mars blockage, but also because the Mars Devil is generally the strongest and most influential devil?"

"Who could have more power than the devil of hate?"

"Hm ... yes ... nothing does more damage than hatred ... ... I didn't expect the devil to have a 'character focus' – I thought there were just the many polar deviations from the sane states ... but hatred is indeed the most destructive element ... and it is

114

most violent in Scorpio because Scorpio is generally the most violent ..."

"Hitler was Taurus with Libra ascendant ..."

"Hm ... o.k. ... but Napoleon was Leo with Scorpio ascendant ..."

"But also Stalin or Goebbels didn't have Scorpio ascendant ... Don't reduce the devil to Scorpio!"

"I'm not doing that at all! I only notice again and again that one or the other characteristic of the devil, that is of you, fits to the zodiac sign Scorpio – especially to the Scorpio Ascendant."

"This is because Scorpio polarizes and because it always lives as intensely as possible – and the Devil is a polarization and an intense image. Moreover, Scorpio is the Mars/Pluto sign – and Pluto corresponds to Kether and Mars corresponds to Geburah. Thus, the devil is depicted Scorpionically and he often looks like a man with Scorpio Ascendant, but that doesn't mean that only people with Scorpio Ascendant can behave like devils."

"O.k., the reasoning makes sense to me. ... ... Thank you, devil."

"You're welcome."

"Ho!"

25.   The Devil in the Tarot

The 15th tarot card may be the best known representation of the devil. Since it appears together with the other 77 tarot cards, this image has contributed a little to make the devil "one image among many others", i.e. to integrate him to some extent.

In the meantime even an article about this card has appeared in the women's magazine "Brigitte", which clearly shows that the fear of the devil has already become much less …

The depiction of the devil is often based on the classic depiction of the devil Baphomet by Eliphas Levi. Baphomet is said to have been honored by the Templars.

The best known is the Rider/Waite tarot from 1910, which most later tarot versions have been based on.

The Devil in the Tarot

Baphomet (by Eliphas Levi)   *The Devil (by Rider/Waite)*

The Tarot card "The Devil" has a multi-layered meaning:

- The devil is what you fear - he is your own shadow.

- The devil is the collective shadow.

- The devil has the legs, head and horns of a goat – he is Pan, which in this context is usually understood as the unbridled sexuality.

- The man and the woman have horns and a tail and are tied to the seat of the devil: they are "animals" and are trapped in the instincts and sexuality that the devil represents (from the Christian point of view).

- The fruit at the end of the woman's tail is fertility and the fire at the end of the man's tail is virility.

- The devil sometimes has women's breasts, i.e. he is a hermaphrodite, a male/female hybrid.

- He points up with his right arm and down with his left arm. This gesture can be found already 25,000 years ago in the late Old Stone Age and also 12,000 years ago at the beginning of the New Stone Age in the temples of Göbekli Tepe in the representations of the mother goddess. This gesture is quite certainly a reference to this world and the hereafter, to body and soul. In connection with the devil, this gesture can be interpreted in various ways: as a reference to the judgment of the afterlife, to magic, to the devil's sphere of influence, etc.

- The inscription "solve et coagula" on his forearms in the depiction of Baphomet are the motto of alchemy: "to solve and to bind". With it the two phases of a transformation are meant. In the Christian sense, this would be a reference to death and the afterlife judgment.

- The position of the hands in the oath gesture shows that the represented is important and reliable.

- The wings indicate that he is an angel. The replacement of the feather wings with bat wings marks him as a fallen, that is, apostate angel.

- The pentagram on the forehead, when it is with one point up, is the symbol of the dominion of the spirit over the body - when it is with one point down, it symbolizes the imprisonment of the spirit in the body. Both can also be understood as incarnation into the world (point down, "coagula") and salvation/enlightenment/paradise (point up, "solve").

117

- The hermes staff between the legs is the kundalini, which rises in the Sushumna (straight staff) and in Ida and Pingala (two serpents). The Kundalini is the surest way to meet and integrate one's own shadow and thus the personal devil.

- The center of the "circle with scales" on the devil's belly is probably in the root chakra – from there the kundalini rises.

- The torch with the three peaks on its head is probably the Kundalini rising. The three points could be the trinity. The torch pointing downwards is a symbol for the incarnation by sexuality.

- The sphere or the ground at the bottom is the earth – this world.

- The devil sits on a seat, that is simultaneously an altar an a throne.

- The cube or double cube (the height is twice the length and the width) on which the devil sits is also a symbol of the tree of life (the double cube has 10 squares as its surface – the tree of life has ten sephiroth plus Da'ath).

- The black and white crescent moons, like the alchemist's saying "solve et coagula" and like the posture of the arms, are an indication that everything moves in polarities and thus in cycles.

- The black background indicates that the devil is in the shadow area.

It is noticeable that the symbolism of the accuser, the torturer and executioner, as well as that of the rebel are missing here. The focus is on sexuality and the cycle of birth and death connected with it, as well as the contrast of trauma formation and enlightenment.

25th Dream Journey to the Devil

"Do you find my interpretation suitable, devil?"
"You have interpreted the images well."
"Hm ... and the images – are they suitable to describe your nature?"
"A bit cerebral and philosophical ... at least the Baphomet ..."
"I can hear my magic teacher Axel protesting loudly ... he doesn't see it that way ... He sees the Kundalini, the connection of light and shadow, the eternal mystery ..."
"That also fits him, doesn't it?"
"Yes, it fits ... ... I noticed that you are, so to speak, my Adi Guru, that is, my root

118

Guru: Axel taught me the basics of magic, and he himself came to magic through the two Tarot cards 'Death' and 'Devil' ..."

"What do you want to say by this?"

"That was actually meant more as an anecdote ..."

"That's another part of your shadow: it's difficult for you to recognize the essential and really align yourself completely with it ..."

"I also have joy in diversity ..."

"And you let yourself be distracted all too often by the variety from your golden thread."

"Um ..."

"There is nothing to say against the joy of variety ... but if you want to become healed and for that you have chosen Kundalini meditation and then you write books about becoming healed and for that you then neglect your meditations – is that effective?"

"No ... it's not ... I've noticed that too ... but sometimes it's not so easy to always stay clearly aligned and on the most effective path ..."

"I'm not accusing you of that as an 'accuser' – I'm just pointing out that sometimes you don't do what you know will get you where you want to go."

"Is that the function of the devil? Making you aware that you've strayed from the path you've chosen for yourself?"

"It is not my function – I am who I am. I am not a function and I do not exist because I have a function. But if you want it, you can use me in that function."

"I am just wondering ... what you are saying sounds just like some of the things in the book 'Conversations with God' ..."

"Everything that comes from the realm of deities sounds similar because it is born of unhindered insight – in the realm of deities there are no delimitations and consequently no limitations of insight."

"Um ... yes ... only this is still a bit unusual for me in the context of the devil ... I mean, to think of the devil as a very 'normal' deity ..."

"You're getting closer to that – and it's doing you decidedly good."

"Yes, that's right. Thank you very much!"

"You're welcome."

"Ho!"

26. The Devil and Black Magic

Actually, there is no Black Magic and just as little White Magic – there is magic, of course, but magic in itself is as neutral as a hammer. However, you can hit a nail with a hammer or you can hit a head with a hammer – the difference arises only by the way of using the hammer or the magic. The techniques in magic are the same everywhere – only the motivations as the basis on which one uses magic differ.

In addition, magic with completely "evil" motivation is just as rare as magic with completely "good" motivation. Therefore, one usually finds no White Magic and also no Black Magic, but only "Gray Magic" – sometimes a bit more light gray, sometimes a bit more dark gray …

Magic itself is neutral, but the magic used is as light or dark as the people who use it. Therefore there is no "devil-magic" and no "God-magic", but only magic in different contexts.

Of course, within a particular civilization, culture, religion, or other group, there is more or less agreement on what use of magic one would call "black magic" – but that mainly says something about the ethics and moral principles and generally the code of conduct in that community.

Since the devil is the unwanted and the undesirable behavior within a community, it is natural to say that the particular scope of magic called "black magic" is the "magic of the devil". Therefore, it is not surprising if black magic is associated with the devil, allegedly practiced by him, that he seduces people into black magic, that the devil is invoked as a helper in black magic, that he is worshipped as a deity in black magic, and so on.

Of course, magic as the ability to cause effects in a non-physical way is especially suspect to be practiced by the devil and devil worshippers. After all, the motivations of these devil-worshippers are by definition evil, and evil acts are punishable. Since magic is not as easy to prove as a physical act, it is obvious that the devil worshippers use magic for their "evil" goals (or at least they are said to do so) to avoid being caught, convicted and punished by the "good guys". Thus magic tends to have a connection with the underground, with the hidden, with the repressed, with the lawbreakers, with the criminals, with the rebels, with the shadow and thus also with the devil.

26th Dream Journey to the Devil

"Did I miss something essential there, devil?"
"No."
"Yes ... good ... thank you! ... ... Ho!"

120

27. The Black Mass

A Black Mass, as the name implies, is based on the Christian Mass. However, it has been turned "black", i.e. from the usual "light-filled" and therefore "White Mass" into its opposite, i.e. into a "Black Mass".

This is also shown quite concretely in the structure of a Black Mass:

- The cross is turned upside down.

- The pentagram is used with the point downwards. (The pentagram is not a Christian sign, of course, but the pentagram with a point down is an anti-Christian symbol).

- The Lord's Prayer is read backwards.

- Instead of Jesus Christ, the devil is invoked.

- On the altar, instead of a host and the communion cup, there is a naked woman.

- Instead of eating the host and drinking the wine, the ritual participants have sex with the woman.

This basic structure of the Black Mass can still be extended at will by all sorts of additions in the same style.

A Black Mass is therefore an anti-Mass, and the devil invoked in it is literally an anti-Christ. Consequently, the point of reference remains Christianity. The participants of a Black Mass are thus very much related to Christianity, but they reject it and express this precisely by the Black Mass.

The "White Mass" and the "Black Mass" are two opposing poles that are distinctly hostile to each other, and each considers the other pole to be "evil" – "evil" in the sense of what the participants in these two types of Mass themselves vehemently reject.

You could also say that in a Black Mass the participants identify with the collectiv shadow.

Here a brief consideration of another subject is necessary:

If one takes a closer look at the processes involved in a healing, one can see that there is almost always a certain dynamic to be found, consisting of several steps in pretty much always the same order:

- A man is trapped in a certain pattern of behavior, e.g. in the role of the victim. This man vehemently rejects the role of the perpetrator as the source of all evil – the perpetrator is the devil to him.

- The man sees that the victim and the perpetrator are the two extremes of the same polarization: the original strength has become power, with the perpetrator striving for more and more power and the victim avoiding any power. This allows the man to see the interdependence of the perpetrator and the victim.
This is the "looking".

- The man either finds the courage to become a perpetrator himself at some point, or he unintentionally becomes a perpetrator when his own repressed anger bursts out of them. In this way, hr experiences the antithesis of his victim role in a very concrete way: he temporarily switches to the perpetrator role.

- When this man has switched back and forth between the victim role and the perpetrator role often enough, he can also experience the behavior of the perpetrator quite consciously and gradually the black and white picture he previously had of victim and perpetrator dissolves. He can now recognize both of them as sufferers, whose character has emerged from the biography of both of them.
This is the "feeling."

- With time, the victim-feelings calm down in this man, because he often also takes on the role of the perpetrator. As a result, more and more pressure is removed from these two roles, so that both the victim role and the perpetrator role shrink: the behaviors in these two roles become less and less extreme. The behavior gradually approaches the middle between these two poles.

- Eventually, the man gets back to his own center – he is then no longer a victim or a perpetrator, but is simply strong and at rest within himself. The power of the perpetrator and the powerlessness of the victim has then become the strength of the sovereign person again.
This is the "embracing."

Thus, the Black Mass can be a necessary and right step on the way of healing a fixation on Christianity or a way out of the role of "victim of Christianity".

However, the Black Mass will almost certainly not be the end point of a healing or of a general worldview development – after all, the Black Mass is primarily the counter-extreme to the normal "White Mass."

The end point of a healing is characterized by the three basic whole qualities of abundance, strength and self-love.

This can then take the most diverse forms – a free Christianity, Zen, Shamanism, Pan-Cult, Wicca or whatever …

27th Dream Journey to the Devil

"Hello devil – from your point of view, have I recognized everything that is signifi-cant for the Black Mass?"

"You describe it quite calmly and matter-of-factly, but the feeling of people on this subject are usually quite violent ..."

"Um ... then what would be a more appropriate way to deal with this issue?"

"Recommending that readers attend a Black Mass?"

"I saw you grinning while you said that! But of course you are a bit right about it – if one wants to experience it, one should do it ... and afterwards one has a clearer opinion about it ... I had, when I once held a magic seminar together with others at Lockenhaus Castle in Austria years ago, the possibility to take part in a Black Mass there, but I refused – I didn't see any sense in taking part in it ... I have a quite relaxed relationship to Christianity and likewise to many other religions ... Therefore, taking part in a Black Mass would have been of no use for me .. "

"You had another idea earlier ..."

"Yes: to invite Christ to a three-way conversation ..."

"And?"

"I thought it would fit better with the next chapter ..."

"Why don't you stop putting your book first – always follow what is most important! You have already described the principle of healing a polarization in this chapter here, although according to your concept this would have rather belonged to the following chapter. ... So go ahead!"

"Yes, well ... You are right ... ... I feel that I have almost more inhibitions to invite Christ into this dream journey than I have had to invite you, devil ..."

"Well – if you have a strained relationship with the devil, you usually have a strained relationship with Christ if you're Christian, or with Moses if you're Jewish, or with Mohammed if Islam is your religion ..."

"All right ... ... Christ – would you like to join us in this dream journey?"

Christ: "Yes – with pleasure."

... ... hm ... the two greet each other kindly ... ...

Christ: "Why not? ... We have known each other for a long time ... And you humans are responsible for the enmities ... There are no enmities in the realm of deities ... For that there would have to be demarcations ... and they don't exist here ..."

Me: "Hm ... now this is a very simple and direct explanation ... but it completely corresponds to what I have experienced with deities so far ... yes ... and also what others have told me about their experiences with deities so far ... ... So enmities among deities exist only in our myths and in our religions, but not among the deities themselves – look at that ... ...

Now I should probably ask the wise questions, if I'm already here together with you two ... but actually ... when I see you there next to each other like that ... I actually can't think of any more questions ... Can you tell me something about it?"

... ...

Devil: "Yes – look at Christ ... do you notice anything about his life course ..."

Me: "Well, the most extreme is the crucifixion ... and the church everywhere depicts these crucifixes, this death ... you can't depict the attitude of the victim more drastically ... and then this symbolism of the sacrificial lamb and 'Lamb of God' and so on ... it's all not too martial and it all doesn't have too much bite, no ... um ... ..."

Christ: "Yes ... and when you look at the devil?"

... ...

Me: "He's the model of the perpetrator ... he's evil, he's aggressive, he's violently emotional ... ... um – look at that ... I've never looked at that in combination ... ... Then what does the wholy state look like??? ... ... well ..."

Christ: "You have developed a ritual, how you can reunite two polarized images – like you do in your ritual for the relationship mandala ..."

Me: "Whew! ... I'm supposed to do that now ... with you? ... ..."

Christ: "Why not?"

... ...

Me: "Whew! ... Now that feels really heavy! ... ... I am supposed to dissolve and transform Christ and the Devil into each other? ... ... yes ... well ... oh boy! ..."

... ...

I now place here before me (in my imagination) a cube ... on the upper side of the cube is a small, flat, round depression ... and on it now stands a large, glassy, semi-transparent egg ... just as the alchemists use it to unite the two primordial opposites Sulphur and Mercurius with each other ....

The glass egg can be opened ... and I now ask Christ and the devil to both go into this glass, to sit down in it ... ... that's what they do ... ... Christ laughs, because he touches the glass with his halo, and the devil laughs, because he obviously has to get his long tail into it somehow, so that the glass can be closed ...

124

... ...

Er ... yes ... well ... oh boy! ... ... this cube with the glass egg is the Athanor of the alchemists, so the alchemical oven ... in there nothing is welded in a physical way or cooked in a chemical way, but something is hatched in a biological way ...

I am now calling up the kundalini from the center of the earth, from the iron/nickel core of the earth, which is its root chakra ... so that the kundalini fire rises ... into this glass egg ... and what is in the glass egg ... is filled with life force ... with so much life force that all ... solidified forms, all extreme forms, all distorted forms, all spasms, and also all traumas – for these are, so to speak, psychic spasms ... dissolve again ... so that what is inside the glass egg is hatched ...

Good – that's what I'm doing now ... ... I'm saying the word 'fire' as a mantra inside as I do in my Kundalini meditations ... the lower end of the egg is its root chakra, so to speak, and the upper, more pointed end is the crown chakra of this egg ... ...

I see a movement in this egg ... but astonishingly little movement ... much less than when I dissolve a normal polarity ... usually there is virtually a fight of the two poles against each other, which destroy and dissolve each other ... this is also described in alchemy ... ...

Um ... maybe more life force fire? ... let's see ... ... well – now I realize, there is something happening ... but it is still astonishing, how little movement there is ... it is almost as if Christ and the Devil both ... would virtually wish this dissolution ...

If you heal e.g. your own distorted image of man, you have e.g. the he-addict and the he-ascetic in the glass egg and they fight fiercely with each other and kill and dismember each other – that is not the case here, there is no fight ... ...

It also doesn't get as dark in the egg as I usually know it, so ... what is called 'caput corvi', the 'raven head' phase with the alchemists ... where the opposites have completely dissolved each other ... and so to speak only black compost is left ... I'll continue with the Kundalini ... ...

Now the color has become uniform ... I see it sometimes as black and sometimes as gray ... hm ... actually black is common here – that's why it's called 'raven's head' – but maybe I see gray here, because this is the middle between the white of Christ and the black of the Devil ...

Then ... now I call the sky-light ... so Bindhu ... what is called in the Indian Upanishads 'milking the sky-cow' ... like in the Kabbalistic 'Exercise of the Middle Pillar' ... this glistening-white light from above I call ... into this egg ... so the Kundalini fire from the earth flows from below through the root chakra of the egg into the egg, and the white light from the sky through the top of the egg, so through the crown chakra of the egg into the egg ... the fire dissolves the old forms and the light reminds the dissolved parts of the original, whole form ...

And while I am telling all this, a lot is already happening here ... ... um ... I hear inwardly the name 'Adam Kadmon' ... in Kabbalah this is the name for the original, whole human being or for the human being who has become healed again ... for the enlightened one, so to speak ... ...

I call again light into the egg – I have the feeling that this is not quite finished yet ... the sky light reminds what is in the egg of its original, whole form ... ... um ... I can guess how in this gray ... the seven main chakras are formed ... this looks really beautiful ... quite a lot of light and color and above all also quite a lot of power ... ... um ... ...

There is something like rays forming from the center of the egg to the outside, but now these are not rays of light, but like ... yes ... as if one would paint very fine wavy lines of light from the inside to the outside on a colour-picture with a very sharp pencil ... as one finds it on some Buddha pictures in the aura of Buddha ... I also know this from some visions – there sometimes such rays appear in the light ...

What is that? ... There was a sound – somewhere between gong and kettledrum? ... yes, but somehow softer ... yes, softer and at the same time, strangely enough, also more powerful ... I have never heard anything like that before in this ritual ... a magic 'egg timer', if I may put it so sloppy ...

I think it means that the contents of the egg are ready, so ...

Me: "When you are finished hatching, contents of this egg ... then open the egg."

... ...

Oh, now there's that weird effect again that sometimes occurs when I do this ritual: the egg just like disappears ... the egg, that is, the glass shell around the contents, just dissolves ...

There's fog that slowly clears and there's a figure ... it reminds me a bit of the scene from the movie 'Age of Ultron', when Ultron came out of his box at the very beginning after he was created ...

He is standing there now ... this figure, I mean ... this is mainly a presence ... so there is something like a consciousness there ... I can perceive the chakras ... I know that this is a human being, and this is ... the primal man, the primal giant yes ... the Germanic people call him Ymir ... the Persians call him Yima ... the Indians call him Yama ... the Jews call him Adam ... the Egyptians call him Atum ... it's all the same primal word ... so it's nostratic, that means Neolithic-Mesopotamian 'Erdom', i.e. 'earth-man', 'earthling' ... that is also the Chinese Pan Gu, the primeval giant ...

Me: "That means ... that is the archetype of the whole man?"

Primordial Man: "Yes."

... ...

"Can I call you by a name?"

"Take 'Pan Gu' ... only few of you know it – that's why it's quite neutral ... and it's also somewhat neutral in Chinese mythology ... i.e. it's not polarized ... except in Yin

and Yang – but that's another kind of polarization, that's only this world and the next, body and soul ..."

"Um ... ... if you are the archetype of the healed human being ... then it seems to me that it would make sense if I connect with you, if I approach you, if you come into me ... ..."

"Yes ... that's exactly it ... as the archetype, I am the origin ... of your image ... I am the origin of what a human being is ... I am the origin of the image of a human ..."

"Um ... that is again another kind of orientation than when I find my soul and then find out, yes, from which sea of a deity my soul is a drop, so to speak ... and this deity is again an aspect of the unity of Kether ... this deity shows the quality of my soul ... but you are somehow different from this ... you don't show me what is special about me as a human being – you show me what is general about me as a human being ... and that is the whole general image of man ... um – up to now I haven't even had the idea to search for such a thing ...

Can you tell me, Pan Gu, when and in what way it makes most sense for me to connect with you?"

"Just come here to me – we'll just become one. ... I am much greater than you, of course, because I am the archetype of all human beings ... but we two still become one."

"Yes, well, deities, as you know, can be in many places at the same time ... then I can unite with You ... and You are also in eight billion other places at the same time – that is, with all other people ... when people see You ... well ...

You come closer and closer ... I see You closer and closer in front of me ... whereas I see You now like a weak light scheme and in there I still see the seven main chakras, which are colorful ... hm ... shining? ... glittering? ... yes, it's something like a 'soft glittering' ... yes, whereas I'm also starting to see the secondary chakras in the hands, the feet, the knees and so on ... and all the nadis ... the acupuncture lines and so on ... I see the life force body, so to speak ... I've never seen it like this before ..."

"Come here."

... ...

I go into it ... yes, into this light glittering light-scheme with the colorful shining chakras ... ...

Each chakra of Pan Gu moves to the place where the corresponding chakra is with me ... and then it is as if ... yes, I would say now, as if something would snap into place, but that is not mechanical, but organic ... there is something joining together ... connecting ....

Phew! ... That feels good! ... ... it's not very spectacular, but it's ... wide ... sincere, upright ... dense ... wholesome ... organic, malleable ... elegant ... beautiful ... hm ... these are all qualities of the center ... there's also a force, but it's ... yes, what's it like? ... relaxed-elastic ... yes, you could call it that ...

127

I feel my third eye – there is this light pulsating pressure ... ...
"Is there ... anything left to do?" ...
"No ... just be ..."
"Yes, well ... er ... thank you very much!"

There comes ... yes, how should I say this now? ... from Pan Gu, but that means also out of myself fullness, strength and smiling ... such a self-love, warmth, such a fulfilment ...

I have to laugh – simply because it feels so good ... ...

"Oh - that feels good! ... That feels good! ... Thank you very, very much! ... ... Ho!"

28. The Chöd Ritual

There are hardly any rituals with the help of which one's own shadow, i.e. the devil can be integrated. One can of course design a unification of these good/evil polarized opposites based on the Sephiroth and Qliphoth of the Tree of Life, but the only known traditional ritual of this kind known to me is the Tibetan Chöd Ritual, whose name means "to cut off" in the sense of "to cut off the ego" – which today one would probably rather paraphrase "to dissolve the ego".

This ritual, which can take quite a few different forms, has two essential elements:

> - One seeks out places one fears such as cemeteries or corpse-burning sites and stays there for extended periods of time, meditating and sleeping there as well.

> - One offers one's own body to the spirits and demons to eat.

In essence, one is ready for what one fears the most: One is ready to die.

The origins of this ritual lie in the initiation journey of the shamans. In several cultures it is described how the shaman on his afterlife journey is killed by demons, man-eaters and the like, cut into pieces, thrown into a cauldron and cooked in it. Often additionally either rock crystals or pieces of iron are thrown into the cauldron. Afterwards the shaman is reassembled from his dismembered body together with the rock crystals or iron pieces.

Since the rock crystals were regarded as parts of the sky (they are transparent like the air) and also the iron pieces (from the iron meteorites one concluded that the sky dome was made of iron), the body of the shaman was afterwards partly earthly and partly "heavenly", i.e. made of the substance of the beyond.

The dismembering itself originates from the tradition to eat some of the more important dead, to keep thier life force inside the tribe – this is the origin of cannibalism.

Such processes of dismembering one's own body and ots putting together afterwards can still be experienced today in dreams and on dream journeys – even without knowing anything about this symbolism.

If one wants to perform a ritual in which one integrates something repressed, one should symbolically dismember both oneself and the repressed, cook it together in a cauldron and then put it together again.

When I was about 28 years old, I dreamt that a "man-eater", who looked like a Neanderthal, cut me and himself into pieces and threw them into a cauldron and cooked them. After a while (when we were "cooked") we came out of the cauldron as one single, clearly healed figure.

This scene has become more famous again, among other things, because of the rebirth of "Lord Voldemort" in the fourth "Harry Potter" volume.

If you want to perform such a ritual yourself, you should see what you want to integrate and design the scenery of the ritual according to your own imagery. This ritual and this scenery should correspond to one's own personal devil.

The alchemical symbolism in the previous dream journey also corresponds to this symbolism: the cauldron is a variant of the alchemical egg.

28th Dream Journey to the Devil

"Do you want to say anything else about this ritual, devil?"

"First, make a dream journey to find your greatest fear. Then build the ritual around that fear. Make the ritual simple and impressive. Include a witness and say all the things you find terrible. And take small steps – there's no point in trying to traumatize yourself by doing things you don't really want to do.

Don't just attend a Black Mass or go to church for the Eucharist if you find it horrible. Look at why you find it terrible – don't worry about the people and things on the outside that have brought you to your attitude, but worry about the images on the inside – those need to be healed."

"You sound like myself, devil ..."

"After all, I'm speaking through you now, and we have the same concern right now – so it's not surprising if you would say similar things to what I'm saying ..."

"That's almost a compliment ..."

"You can take it that way if you want ..."

"Thank you."

"You're welcome."

"Ho!"

29. Tabular Curriculum Vitae of the devil

You can now make a tabular curriculum vitae of the devil, that is, show the development of his character. For many developments there is only very approximate time information, but for a rough overview what is known about the devil is quite sufficient.

The Personal Data Sheet of the Devil											
-10000 to -9000	-9000 to -8000	-8000 to -7000	-7000 to -6000	-6000 to -5000	-5000 to -4000	-4000 to -3000	-3000 to -2000	-2000 to -1000	-1000 to 0	0 to +1000	+1000 to +2000
wilderness god											
herd-animal reprocreation symbolism											
		killer of the corn god = reaper									
		Heyoka (actor of anti-righteousness)									
						god of anti-righteousness					
						executioner at the afterlife court					
						god of the foreign peoples					
							prosecutor at the beyond court				
							herd-animal god				
							rebel				
								God's enemy			
								ruler of the dead			
								devil's grandmother			
								hellhound			
									mound hell		
									Anti-Christ		
									seducer		
									sex demon		
											shadow

Apart from the role of the wilderness god, which has faded in the meantime because there is not much wilderness left on earth, all known aspects of the devil have survived into today's image of the devil.

29th Dream Journey to the Devil

"Do you find this representation accurate, devil?"
"Add the concept of the shadow – that is still missing."

I have entered it into this overview afterwards.

"Anything else?"
"No."
"Then this is now a biography authorized by you, so to speak?"
"If you enjoy calling it that – yes."
"Thank you."
"You're welcome."
"Ho!"

30. Sympathy for the Devil

The song "Sympathy for the Devil" is quite certainly the most famous "hymn to the devil".

This song was written by the Rolling Stones and contains some interesting verses:

> *Please allow me to introduce myself*
> *I'm a man of wealth and taste*
> *I've been around for a long, long years*
> *Stole million man's soul an faith*

Stealing souls by causing people to sin is something the devil is commonly accused of.

> *And I was 'round when Jesus Christ*
> *Had his moment of doubt and pain*
> *Made damn sure that Pilate*
> *Washed his hands and sealed his fate*

> *Pleased to meet you*
> *Hope you guess my name*
> *But what's puzzling you*
> *Is the nature of my game*

I have tried to get to the bottom of the mystery of the devil's nature and "game" in this book …

> *Stuck around St. Petersburg*
> *When I saw it was a time for a change*
> *Killed Tsar and his ministers*
> *Anastasia screamed in vain*

> *I rode a tank*
> *Held a general's rank*
> *When the blitzkrieg raged*
> *And the bodies stank*

The devil is said to cause wars and revolutions and murders …

Pleased to meet you
Hope you guess my name, oh yeah
Ah, what's puzzling you
Is the nature of my game, oh yeah

I watched with glee
While your kings and queens
Fought for ten decades
For the gods they made

The rulers fight for the ideals they themselves have created – and thereby create a collective devil.

I shouted out
Who killed the Kennedys?
When after all
It was you and me

Here the devil says that not he alone, but he and those who are listening to him, killed the Kennedys – the people create the suffering and the devil is either the one who drives the people to it, or simply the image in the people of this suffering and of these assassinations …

Let me please introduce myself
I'm a man of wealth and taste
And I laid traps for troubadours
Who get killed before they reached Bombay

Pleased to meet you
Hope you guessed my name, oh yeah
But what's puzzling you
Is the nature of my game, oh yeah, get down, baby

This is either an allusion to sex, which is also part of the devil (and the Rolling Stones), or an invitation to submit to the devil.

Pleased to meet you
Hope you guessed my name, oh yeah
But what's confusing you
Is just the nature of my game

Just as every cop is a criminal
And all the sinners saints
As heads is tails
Just call me Lucifer
'Cause I'm in need of some restraint

This could be interpreted as Lucifer saying here that what is good and what is evil is first determined by man – who or what the devil is is determined by man himself.

So if you meet me
Have some courtesy
Have some sympathy, and some taste
Use all your well-learned politnesse
Or I'll lay your soul to waste, mm yeah

Pleased to meet you
Hope you guessed my name, mm yeah
But what's puzzling you
Is the nature of my game, mm mean it, get down

Here you will find the classic threat to the soul …

Woo, who
Oh yeah, get on down
Oh yeah
Aah yeah

But what confuses you
Is the meaning of my game, mm
I'm serious, down with you!
Woo, woo, oh yes, down with you!

Here the devil is asked to kneel down before him, i.e. to submit to his will.

Tell me baby, what's my name?
Tell me honey, can ya guess my name?
Tell me baby, what's my name?
I tell you one time, you're to blame

Here Lucifer says once again that the people are to blame and not the devil.

What's my name
Tell me, baby, what's my name?
Tell me, sweetie, what's my name?

This song is amazingly substantial … and of course it fits well with the Rolling Stones, who cultivated the image of rebels – as opposed to the Beatles, who were the "good boys."

30th Dream Journey to the Devil

"Well, Devil – now I've come to the end of this book … this is your last chance to say anything else that will go into this book …"
"Better say 'the last chance for me to get something from you that will make my book more interesting' …"
"All right …"
"Mañana."
"Mañana … tomorrow? Do you want me to take this last dream trip tomorrow?"
"Yes."
"Yes, alrigth – then see you tomorrow."
"See you tomorrow."
"Ho!"

The next morning:

"Hello Devil … since I have no more questions, I'd like to leave it up to you to decide if there's anything else you'd like to say – and if so, what."
"Dream."
"What do you mean by 'dreaming'?"
"The day dreaming – the night dreaming will follow."

"Why should I daydream ... and about what?"

"About what you actually are, about what you want to express, and about what you want to experience."

"Hm, that this makes sense I can already see, but what does this have to do with you?"

"I am what you do not desire."

"Hm ... yes ... we've already talked about that ... If I don't choose anything, nothing happens – at least I don't get to things I've wished for ..."

"By dreaming you come to a vision of what you want to radiate, be and experience."

"My identity is in my heart chakra ... and daydreaming of what I want to be, radiate and experience is in my solar plexus and in my throat chakra ... Are you recommending daydreaming, feeling, because my throat chakra has been blocked?"

"Yes – but not only your throat chakra, but also your heart chakra and your wish tree have been blocked."

"Yes, those have been the main issues in my Kundalini meditations. ... Is wish dreaming what's next now? Realizing what I most want to have in my life?"

"Yes – why are you healing yourself and why are you clearing your chakras if you don't start to shine afterwards?"

"So dreaming is the next step after the healing, after the integration of Christ and Devil ... and after that comes the concretization of the desires in the waking consciousness in the hara and in the third eye ... and then the experience in ecstasy, that is in onepointedness in the root chakra and in the crown chakra ... and the starting point for all this is my identity, my soul in my heart chakra – that is the deep sleep ....

Yes, it makes sense to me that after the dissolution of the blockages, dreaming is the most important thing ... I would not have come to this as quickly on my own ...

To dream my ideal life out of my heart chakra in my solar plexus and in my throat chakra ... yes, that makes sense to me ...

Whereby the knowledge about what happens in which chakra is not the central point – even if this helps me personally and gives orientation ...

Thank you very much!"

"You're welcome."

"Is there anything else to say?"

"No – not right now. But I'll be in touch if anything ever comes up ... or just come and see me ..."

"Yes, o.k. ... thank you very much!"

"You're welcome."

"Ho!"

English Books by Harry Eilenstein

- Living Magic (261 p.)	- Money Magic for Beginners (60 p.)
- The Synthesis of Physics and Magic (192 p.)	- Magic Objects for Beginners (64 p.)
- Telepathy for Beginners (60 p.)	- Shamanism for Beginners (52 p.)
- Telepathy for Advanced Learners (52 p.)	- Chakra-Magic for Beginners (148 p.)
- Telekinesis for Beginners (56 p.)	- Language of the Moon – for Beginners (128 p.)
- Life Force for Beginners (76 p.)	- Self Knowledge for Beginners (60 p.)
- Kundalini for Beginners (104 p.)	- Da'ath-Magic for Beginners (64 p.)
- Astral Projection for Beginners (60 p.)	- Astrology for Beginners (112 p.)
- Meditation for Beginners (60 p.)	- Number Symbolism for Beginners (64 p.)
- Prophecy for Beginners (60 p.)	- Mandalas for Beginners (76 p.)
- Ritual Magic for Beginners (64 p.)	- Crop Circles for Beginners (344 p.)
- Magic Chant for Beginners (108 p.)	- Feng Shui for Beginners (96 p.)
- Invocations for Beginners (52 p.)	- Magic Research for Beginners (140 p.)
- Evocations for Beginners (62 p.)	
- Auto-Movement for Beginners (60 p.)	- Magic for Beginners – Anthology I (636 p.)
- Elves for Beginners (56 p.)	- Magic for Beginners – Anthology II (616 p.)
- Hypnosis for Beginners (56 p.)	- Magic for Beginners – Anthology III (684 p.)
- Love Magic for Beginners (52 p.)	- Magic for Beginners – Anthology IV (580 p.)

Bücher von Harry Eilenstein

Religion allgemein
- Die sieben Schritte des Lebens (428 S.)
- Muttergöttin und Schamanen (168 S.)
- Göbekli Tepe (472 S.)
- Die Göttin von Göbekli Tepe (144 S.)
- Totempfähle (440 S.)
- Der Urriese (168 S.)
- Die Biographie des Teufels (144 S.)
- Pan (336 S.)
- Christus (60 S.)
- Dakini (80 S.)
- Vajra (76 S.)

Ägypten
- Hathor und Re 1: Götter und Mythen im Alten Ägypten (432 S.)
- Hathor und Re 2: Die altägyptische Religion – Ursprünge, Kult und Magie (396 S.)
- Isis (508 S.)

Indogermanen
- Die Entwicklung der indogermanischen Religionen (700 S.)
- Wurzeln und Zweige der indogermanischen Religion (224 S.)

Germanen
- Die Götter der Germanen (87 Bände – siehe nächste Seite)
- Odin (300 S.)

Kelten
- Cernunnos (690 S.)
- Taliesin (228 S.)
- Der Kessel von Gundestrup (220 S.)
- Der Chiemsee-Kessel (76)

Psychologie
- Über die Freude (100 S.)
- Das Geheimnis des inneren Friedens (252 S.)
- Das Beziehungsmandala (52 S.)
- Gefühle und ihre Verwandlungen (404 S.)
- einsgerichtet (140 S.)
- Liebe und Eigenständigkeit (216 S.)
- Von innerer Fülle zu äußerem Gedeihen (52 S.)

Heilung
- Die Symbolik der Krankheiten (76 S.)

Kunst
- Herz des Tanzes – Tanz des Herzens (160 S.)

Drama
- König Athelstan (104 S.)

Bücher von Harry Eilenstein

„Magie für Anfänger"	Magie

„Magie für Anfänger"

- Telepathie für Anfänger (60 S.)
- Telepathie für Fortgeschrittene (52 S.)
- Telekinese für Anfänger (52 S.)
- Lebenskraft für Anfänger (60 S.)
- Meditation für Anfänger (56 S.)
- Kundalini für Anfänger (100 S.)
- Hypnose für Anfänger (56 S.)
- Auto-Movement für Anfänger (56 S.)
- Chakra-Magie für Anfänger (148 S.)
- Astralreisen für Anfänger (56 S.)
- Astrologie für Anfänger (120 S.)
- Ritual-Magie für Anfänger (56 S.)
- Mandalas für Anfänger (68 S.)
- Geldzauber für Anfänger (56 S.)
- Liebeszauber für Anfänger (52 S.)
- Invokationen für Anfänger (52 S.)
- Evokationen für Anfänger (60 S.)
- Elfen für Anfänger (56 S.)
- Magie-Forschung für Anfänger (140 S.)
- Selbsterkenntnis für Anfänger (52 S.)
- Zahlensymbolik für Anfänger (60 S.)
- Die Sprache des Mondes – für Anfänger (116 S.)
- Zaubergesänge für Anfänger (100 S.)
- Zukunftschau für Anfänger (60 S.)
- Schamanismus für Anfänger (52 S.)
- Magische Gegenstände für Anfänger (68 S.)
- Da'ath-Magie für Anfänger (64 S.)
- Kornkreise für Anfänger (348 S.)
- Feng Shui für Anfänger (96 S.)
- Magie für Anfänger – Sammelband I (696 S.)
- Magie für Anfänger – Sammelband II (664 S.)
- Magie für Anfänger – Sammelband III (580 S.)

„Traumreisen"

- Traumreisen zu Heilpflanzen (700 S.)

Magie

- Handbuch für Zauberlehrlinge (408 S.)
- Tarot (104 S.)
- Physik und Magie (184 S.)
- Die Synthese von Physik und Magie (200S.)
- Die Magie-Formel (156 S.)
- Krafttiere – Tiergöttinnen – Tiertänze (112 S.)
- Schwitzhütten (524 S.)
- Mythen und Magie der Harfe (116 S.)
- Magie heute – Berichte aus der Praxis (288 S.)

Meditation

- Der Lebenskraftkörper (230 S.)
- Die Chakren (100 S.)
- Das Chakren-System mit den Nebenchakren (296 S.)
- Organe und Chakren (64 S.)
- Die platonischen Körper in den Chakren (156 S.)
- Meditation (140 S.)
- Drachenfeuer (124 S.)
- Kundalini I (676 S.)
- Reinkarnation (156 S.)
- einsgerichtet (140 S.)

Astrologie

- Astrologie (496 S.)
- Photo-Astrologie (428 S.)
- Die astrologischen Aspekte (88 S.)
- Horoskop und Seele (120 S.)

Kabbala

- Kursus der praktischen Kabbala (150 S.)
- Eltern der Erde (450 S.)
- Blüten des Lebensbaumes:
    - Die Struktur des kabbalistischen Lebensbaumes (370 S.)
    - Der kabbalistische Lebensbaum als Forschungshilfsmittel (580 S.)
    - Der kabbalistische Lebensbaum als spirituelle Landkarte (520 S.)

Die Themen der 87 Bände der Reihe „Die Götter der Germanen"

1. Die Entwicklung der germanischen Religion
2. Lexikon der germanischen Religion
3. Der ursprüngliche Göttervater Tyr
4. Tyr in der Unterwelt: der Schmied Wieland
5. Tyr in der Unterwelt: der Riesenkönig   Teil 1
6. Tyr in der Unterwelt: der Riesenkönig   Teil 2
7. Tyr in der Unterwelt: der Zwergenkönig
8. Der Himmelswächter Heimdall
9. Der Sommergott Baldur
10. Der Meeresgott: Ägir, Hler und Njörd
11. Der Eibengott Ullr
12. Die Zwillingsgötter Alcis
13. Der neue Göttervater Odin   Teil 1
14. Der neue Göttervater Odin   Teil 2
15. Der Fruchtbarkeitsgott Freyr
16. Der Chaos-Gott Loki
17. Der Donnergott Thor
18. Der Priestergott Hönir
19. Die Göttersöhne
20. Die unbekannteren Götter
21. Die Göttermutter Frigg
22. Die Liebesgöttin: Freya und Menglöd
23. Die Erdgöttinnen
24. Die Korngöttin Sif
25. Die Apfel-Göttin Idun
26. Die Hügelgrab-Jenseitsgöttin Hel
27. Die Meeres-Jenseitsgöttin Ran
28. Die unbekannteren Jenseitsgöttinnen
29. Die unbekannteren Göttinnen
30. Die Nornen
31. Die Walküren
32. Die Zwerge
33. Der Urriese Ymir
34. Die Riesen
35. Die Riesinnen
36. Mythologische Wesen
37. Mythologische Priester und Priesterinnen
38. Sigurd/Siegfried
39. Helden und Göttersöhne
40. Die Symbolik der Vögel und Insekten
41. Die Symbolik der Schlangen, Drachen und Ungeheuer
42.a Die Symbolik der Herdentiere I
42.b Die Symbolik der Herdentiere II
43. Die Symbolik der Raubtiere
44. Die Symbolik der Wassertiere und sonstigen Tiere
45. Die Symbolik der Pflanzen
46. Die Symbolik der Farben
47. Die Symbolik der Zahlen
48. Die Symbolik von Sonne, Mond und Sternen
49.a Das Jenseits I – Das Hügelgrab
49.b Das Jenseits II – Der Jenseitsweg
50. Seelenvogel, Utiseta und Einweihung
51. Wiederzeugung und Wiedergeburt
52. Elemente der Kosmologie
53. Der Weltenbaum
54. Die Symbolik der Himmelsrichtungen und der Jahreszeiten
55.a Mythologische Motive I
55.b Mythologische Motive II
56. Der Tempel
57. Die Einrichtung des Tempels
58. Priesterin – Seherin – Zauberin – Hexe
59. Priester – Seher – Zauberer
60. Rituelle Kleidung und Schmuck
61. Skalden und Skaldinnen
62 Kriegerinnen und Ekstase-Krieger
63. Die Symbolik der Körperteile
64.a Magie und Ritual I
64.b Magie und Ritual II
64.c Magie und Ritual III
65. Gestaltwandlungen
66.a Magische Angriffs-Waffen
66.b Magische Verteidigungs-Waffen
67. Magische Werkzeuge und Gegenstände
68. Zaubersprüche
69. Göttermet
70. Zaubertränke
71. Träume, Omen und Orakel
72. Runen
73. Sozial-religiöse Rituale
74. Weisheiten und Sprichworte
75. Kenningar
76. Rätsel
77. Die vollständige Edda des Snorri Sturluson
78. Frühe Skaldenlieder
79.a Mythologische Sagas I
79.b Mythologische Sagas II
80. Hymnen an die germanischen Götter

140